# THANKSGIVING:
## The True Story

# THANKSGIVING:
## The True Story

### PENNY COLMAN

Christy Ottaviano Books
HENRY HOLT AND COMPANY
NEW YORK

Henry Holt and Company, LLC
*Publishers since 1866*
175 Fifth Avenue
New York, New York 10010
www.HenryHoltKids.com

Library of Congress Cataloging-in-Publication Data
Colman, Penny.
Thanksgiving : the true story / Penny Colman.
p.      cm.
Includes bibliographical references.
1. Thanksgiving Day—Juvenile literature.   2. United States—Social life and
customs—Juvenile literature.   I. Title.
ISBN-13: 978-0-8050-8229-6 / ISBN-10: 0-8050-8229-8
GT4975.C55 2008       394.2649—dc22        2007046943

First edition—2008
Printed in the United States of America on acid-free paper. ∞

1   3   5   7   9   10   8   6   4   2

Permission for use of the following is gratefully acknowledged: "The First Thanksgiving Boston,
1631," by Arthur Guiterman. Reprinted by permission of Richard Sclove.

This book is for Linda.

—∽—

# Acknowledgments

I am grateful to many people, including the graduate students at Queens College, the City University of New York, who first piqued my interest in this topic, and the many people who responded to my Thanksgiving survey. Then there are all the people who helped me piece together the true story of Thanksgiving. Lorrie Jones, at the Chamber of Commerce in Canyon, Texas, actually drove along Highway 217 in search of the historic marker for the feast of the first Thanksgiving in 1541. Georgia Holder, president of the National Society Daughters of the American Colonists, generously provided me with information and loaned me primary source materials about the 1541 event in Texas and the 1619 event in Virginia. Fred P. Woodlief III, a direct descendant of Captain John Woodliffe (also spelled Woodlief and Woodleefe) and a former director on the Virginia Thanksgiving Festival board, graciously responded to my request for information. Helene Wolf gave me the materials her parents had brought home from their trip to Berkeley Plantation, Virginia. Ben Sanchez sent me a photograph of the reenactment of the 1598 event in Texas. David Glime, Rod Library, University of

Northern Iowa, located a 1916 advertisement. Norm Scott, Farm Sanctuary, and Susan Addy, Homowo African Arts & Cultures, provided pictures. Sue Kirch shared her expertise in image processing. Jennifer Govan, Gottesman Library, Teachers College, Columbia University, helped me locate historical schoolbooks and curriculum material. Other people answered my questions, including Peggy Baker, director and librarian, Pilgrim Hall Museum, Plymouth, Massachusetts; Andrea Thorpe, library director, Richards Free Library, Newport, New Hampshire; and Linda S. Levstik, professor, Social Studies, University of Kentucky. Dot Emer and Annie Unverzagt distributed my Thanksgiving survey to teenagers. Jan Kristo, professor, Reading and Language Arts, the University of Maine, kept up a lively e-mail exchange, cheering me on as I unraveled the complicated story of Thanksgiving. My son David Lewis-Colman, assistant professor of African American history, Ramapo College of New Jersey, and I spent many hours engaged in stimulating and productive discussions about this book. As always, Linda Hickson provided indispensable support. Once again Christy Ottaviano was an editor extraordinaire. Thank you to her, the people at Henry Holt, and everyone who contributed to the making of this book.

# Contents

PART II ❧ THANKSGIVING TRADITIONS

# THANKSGIVING:
## The True Story

# Author's Note

Thanksgiving is my favorite holiday. Why? Because I love to cook and eat and gather together with family and friends. And I believe in giving thanks. So do the millions of Americans who celebrate Thanksgiving every year on the fourth Thursday in November. My longtime friend Dot Emer, who is a middle school librarian in Boca Raton, Florida, happily recalls many "wonderful dinners and family reunions." Now, Dot says, "I enjoy traveling across the country to California to feast with our daughter and her family and friends. It is a happy family time." Dot's husband, Ralph, says, "It's a wonderful time of year to be with family and friends. We always pray for God's continued blessing, and pray for those in need." Although most Americans today celebrate Thanksgiving, few know the true story of the origins of the holiday.

When I was in school in the 1950s, I learned that the "first" Thanksgiving happened in 1621 in Plymouth, Massachusetts, when the Pilgrims and Indians got together to eat turkey and stuffing and gravy and mashed potatoes and corn and cranberry sauce and pumpkin pie. Years later, in the late 1970s and early 1980s, my children learned the same story. My niece learned this same story in 2003. But is it the true story?

I did not ask that question until recently, when I taught a course in teaching history through literature at Queens College, the City University of New York. That is when I discovered that there is an abundance of books, articles, and Web sites that tell the traditional Thanksgiving story. But there are also books, articles, and Web sites that tell different stories. What is the true story? I wondered. This book is my answer.

In my search, I used a variety of sources. I consulted firsthand reports; Native American accounts; Thanksgiving proclamations by governors and presidents; poetry and folk songs; magazines, including *Godey's Lady's Magazine*, *Harper's Weekly*, and *The Youth's Companion*; newspapers, such as the *New York Times*, *Washington Post*, and *Christian Science Monitor*; journal articles by historians and social scientists; historic markers; online museum and library exhibits; and experts.

As part of my research, I created a survey with a series of questions about what people believed about Thanksgiving and how they celebrated. One hundred thirty-eight people, more than 50 percent of the people I sent it to, returned my survey. They ranged in age from twelve to eighty-nine years old and were racially and ethnically diverse. Women, men, girls, and boys responded from around the country. You'll find some of these responses to my survey throughout this book.

As with my previous books, I did the picture research. I look for images in old books, magazines, and newspapers; in picture collections in museums, archives, and libraries; and in online collections. I am particularly interested in primary source documents and in images that have not been widely reproduced or reproduced at all. I also travel to do my own photography for a book. My trips for this one included attending contemporary harvest festivals and visiting historic sites in Newport, New Hampshire, and Plymouth, Massachusetts.

*Thanksgiving: The True Story* is organized into two parts. Part I is about the origins of the Thanksgiving that we celebrate today. In the first chapter, I examine twelve claims for the location of the "first" Thanksgiving—two in Texas, two in Florida, one in Maine, two in Virginia, and five in Massachusetts. In chapters 2 and 3, I write about the true origins of our Thanksgiving. In chapter 4, I answer the question: What about the "Pilgrim and Indian" Thanksgiving story? In Part II, I focus on Thanksgiving gatherings, activities, food, and meanings.

This is the true story of Thanksgiving—as true as it can be, based on the available evidence. New evidence, of course, might be discovered, or old evidence might be reinterpreted. I am open to that and am hopeful that you are too. Because what we believe matters. It matters because it shapes our identity and actions, as individuals and as a nation.

## PART I

# THANKSGIVING ORIGINS

# ONE

# The "First" Thanksgiving:
# Competing Claims

When I decided to write this book, I was curious about other people's experiences with Thanksgiving. So I sent out a survey to teenagers and adults. The first question asked what they had learned in school. One hundred percent of the teenagers and the majority of adults reported that they had learned what I had learned—that the Pilgrims and Indians celebrated the "first" Thanksgiving in Plymouth, Massachusetts, in 1621. But as I did my research, I discovered that there are many competing claims for the "first" Thanksgiving based on events that happened in Texas, Florida, Maine, Virginia, and Massachusetts.

None of the claims, I should point out, were made by the people involved in the events, but by people who lived many years later. Why would anyone make such a claim? There are multiple reasons, including regional pride—it happened in Virginia, not in Massachusetts; ethnic identity—it was Spanish-speaking people, not English-speaking people; religious identity—it was religious, not secular; it was Catholics, not Protestants.

# Table 1. Competing Claims for the "First" Thanksgiving

| WHEN | WHERE | WHAT | NATURE of the CLAIM (How the Claim Was Made and Promoted) |
|---|---|---|---|
| May 29, 1541 | Palo Duro Canyon in Texas | Thanksgiving Mass to mark finding food and shelter for Francisco Vásquez de Coronado's expedition | • Historical marker placed in 1959 by Texas Society Daughters of American Colonists<br>• Article in 1999 by Max Albright<br>• Thanksgiving Timeline (TT) by the Library of Congress, American Memory |
| June 30, 1564 | La Caroline, near present-day Jacksonville, Florida | Service of Thanksgiving for the safe voyage of French colonists led by René de Laudonnière | • Article by Jerry Wilkinson<br>• TT |
| September 8, 1565 | St. Augustine, Florida | Thanksgiving Mass and feast with the Timucuan Indians for the successful arrival of Pedro Menéndez de Avilés and his troops | • Book in 1965 by Michael Gannon<br>• 1980s media coverage of Gannon's book<br>• Children's nonfiction book in 2007 by Robyn Gioia |
| April 30, 1598 | Near present-day San Elizario, Texas | Ceremony, held by Juan de Oñate's expedition, with a Thanksgiving Mass and a feast with the Manso Indians to commemorate their successful journey | • Annual reenactments since 1989<br>• Articles in 1999 by Pauline Chavez Bent, and in 2003 by Don Adams and Teresa A. Kendrick<br>• *Lonely Planet Texas* travel guide |
| August 19, 1607 | Near present-day Popham Beach, Maine | Service held to mark the safe arrival of English settlers led by George Popham | • Editorial in the *New York Times*, November 28, 1916<br>• Article in 1997 by Ellen Barry<br>• Inclusion in 1985 Presidential Thanksgiving Proclamation<br>• TT |
| 1610 | Jamestown, Virginia | Thanksgiving service held after the arrival of desperately needed supply ships | • TT |

| WHEN | WHERE | WHAT | NATURE of the CLAIM (How the Claim Was Made and Promoted) |
|---|---|---|---|
| 1619 | Berkeley Plantation, Virginia | Service of Thanksgiving for safe arrival of Berkeley Hundred, a group of English colonists led by Captain John Woodleefe | • Dr. Lyon G. Tyler's discovery of original order in early 1900s<br>• Historical plaque erected in 1969 by National Society Daughters of the American Colonists<br>• Virginia State Department of Education–produced film<br>• Inclusion in 1985 Presidential Thanksgiving Proclamation<br>• Annual reenactments |
| 1620 | Provincetown, Massachusetts | Service of Thanksgiving for safe arrival of the *Mayflower* in Provincetown Harbor | • Firsthand report by Elizabeth Reis, who grew up in Provincetown: "We were always told as part of the grade school curriculum that the settlers had Thanksgiving in P-town." |
| 1621 | Plymouth Colony, Massachusetts | Celebration and feast shared by English colonists and Wampanoag after a successful harvest | • Book in 1841 by Alexander Young<br>• Countless claims from the late 1800s to the present day |
| 1623 | Plymouth, Massachusetts | Service of thanksgiving for the rain that ended a drought | • Periodic claims in various publications from the mid-1800s to early 1900s |
| 1630 | Boston, Massachusetts | Service of thanksgiving for safe arrival of colonists | • TT<br>• Periodic claims in various publications from the mid-1800s to early 1900s |
| 1631 | Boston, Massachusetts | Service of thanksgiving for the arrival of desperately needed supplies | • Popular poem in 1933 by Arthur Guiterman<br>• Periodic claims in various publications from early 1800s to mid-1900s |

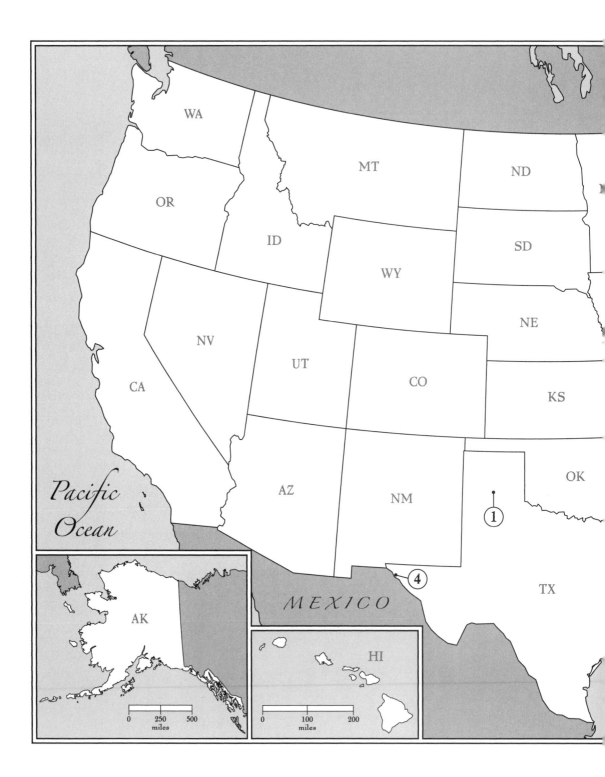

Pacific
Ocean

WA

OR

ID

MT

ND

SD

WY

NV

UT

CO

NE

CA

AZ

NM

KS

OK

1

4

TX

MEXICO

AK

HI

0    250    500
miles

0    100    200
miles

CANADA

Lake Superior

MI

WI

Lake Michigan

Lake Huron

MI

Lake Ontario

Lake Erie

IL

IN

OH

WV

VA

KY

TN

NC

MS

AL

GA

SC

LA

FL

Gulf of Mexico

0     125     250
        miles

ME

VT

NH

MA

CT

RI

NY

PA

NJ

MD

DE

Atlantic
Ocean

⑤

⑪ ⑫

⑨ ⑩

⑧

⑦

⑥

② 

③

## Thanksgiving Claims

① 1541, Palo Duro Canyon (TX)

② 1564, La Caroline (FL)

③ 1565, St. Augustine (FL)

④ 1598, San Elizario (TX)

⑤ 1607, Popham Colony (ME)

⑥ 1610, Jamestown Colony (VA)

⑦ 1619, Berkeley Plantation (VA)

⑧ 1620, Provincetown (MA)

⑨ 1621, Plymouth Colony (MA)

⑩ 1623, Plymouth Colony (MA)

⑪ 1630, Boston (MA)

⑫ 1631, Boston (MA)

## Who Is Right?

So, who is right? To help you think about this question I have made a chart with basic information about each claim (see table 1).

As you look at the chart, you'll see that there are twelve claims: two in Texas, two in Florida, one in Maine, two in Virginia, and five in Massachusetts. You'll also note that all the events had to do with the arrival of something—food, shelter, rain, supplies, or safe arrival at a destination.

In evaluating the claims, I asked this key question: What was the basis for making the claim? The answer, I discovered, is: They are all based on documents or accounts from the original event. Here are three examples of how the claims are connected to a document from the event.

## A Florida Claim

First, let's look at the September 8, 1565, claim. Earlier in the year, King Philip II of Spain had sent Admiral Pedro Menéndez de Avilés to get rid of French colonists who had established a settlement, La Caroline, on the St. John's River near present-day Jacksonville. In late August 1565, Menéndez and hundreds of soldiers arrived on the coast of Florida, and marched with trumpets blaring and banners flying into a Timucuan Indian village. Menéndez turned one of the Timucuans' longhouses into a fort and named the village St. Augustine. Today, St. Augustine is the oldest permanent European settlement on the North American continent.

On September 8, 1565, Menéndez celebrated a Mass of Thanksgiving and invited the Timucuan led by Chief Seloy. After the religious ceremony, they most likely ate hard sea biscuits and *cocido*—a stew made from salted pork and garbanzo beans laced with garlic. Three weeks later, Menéndez led his soldiers for four days through "marsh, forest tangle, fierce winds, and heavy rainfall." After resting one night, Menéndez and his men massacred most of the French.

In 1965, Michael Gannon, a historian at the University of Florida, wrote a scholarly book, *The Cross in the Sand,* which included the story of Menéndez's Thanksgiving Mass and feast based on official documents and reports of the event. Twenty years later, a newspaper reporter wrote about Gannon's account of Menéndez's Thanksgiving and generated a "storm of interest," according to Gannon: "I was on the phone for three days straight." The storm subsided, but not before he was labeled by supporters of the Pilgrim and Indian event in Plymouth as "the Grinch who stole Thanksgiving." In 2007, a fifth-grade teacher, Robyn Gioia, who heard about Menéndez in a workshop led by Gannon, was hoping to stir things up again with the publication of her nonfiction picture book *America's REAL First Thanksgiving: St. Augustine, Florida, September 8, 1565.* "If you want something to be known," says Gioia, "you teach the kids."

Now, let's examine the April 30, 1598, claim. It involves Juan de Oñate, a Spanish explorer, who is credited as the founder of the first European settlements in present-day New Mexico. In January 1598, Oñate set out on a hazardous journey across the Chihuahuan Desert in northern Mexico with more than seven thousand animals and over five hundred men, women, and children, including people from Spain, Greece, Italy, Africa, Cuba, and a few Chichimeca Indian slaves.

After eighty-six harrowing days, the expedition reached the Rio

A group of modern-day people participate in a reenactment in El Paso, Texas, of the "first" Thanksgiving held by Juan de Oñate in 1598.

Bravo, now called the Rio Grande River. With the help of Manso Indians, they found a safe place to cross the river near present-day San Elizario, Texas. That's where Oñate ordered his men to build a church, and on April 30, Fray Alfonso Martínez sang a "very solemn Mass" to give thanks to God. After the Mass, they shared a feast with the Manso Indians. We know all this because Gaspar Pérez de Villagrá, a Spanish poet and a member of Oñate's expedition in 1598, published his firsthand account of the expedition in 1610.

Although Villagrá did not label April 30 as the "first Thanksgiving," hundreds of years later other people did. Pauline Chavez Bent quoted Villagrá in an article she wrote in 1999, "The First Thanksgiving (The Pilgrims Missed It)." So did Don Adams and Teresa A. Kendrick in their 2003 article, "Don Juan de Oñate and the First Thanksgiving." In their authors' note, Adams and Kendrick wrote: "We carefully considered, as we understood it, the original document written by a participant in the expedition." Since 1989, the Mission Trail Association of El Paso, Texas, has held reenactments of the 1598 Thanksgiving.

## A Virginia Claim

The third example of how a claim is connected to a document from the original event is from 1619. Unlike the other claims, this is said to be the "First Official Thanksgiving Day in America." Here is why: The original document is an order from the proprietors,

A modern artist's idea of the first settlers observing the "first" Thanksgiving in 1619. This picture appears in the brochure for Berkeley Plantation, Charles City, Virginia, with the caption "On December 4, 1619, early settlers from England came ashore at Berkeley and observed the first official Thanksgiving in America."

the financial backers, to the English colonists, known as the Berkeley Hundred, who sailed on board the *Margaret* to Virginia. The order read (in modern spelling): WE ORDAIN THAT THE DAY OF OUR SHIP'S ARRIVAL . . . SHALL BE YEARLY AND PERPETUALLY KEPT HOLY AS A DAY OF THANKSGIVING TO ALMIGHTY GOD. Upon their arrival at the present-day site of Berkeley Plantation, the colonists followed orders and observed a day of thanksgiving and prayer. Most likely, they continued the practice until they were attacked by Native Americans and annihilated in 1622.

The Berkeley Hundred had a historian, John Smyth of Nibley, who remained in England. Among the many documents he kept was a copy of the Thanksgiving order. Hundreds of years later, Smyth's records were sold and ended up in the New York Public Library (NYPL) in New York City. In 1899, the library printed *Virginia Papers 1616–1619*, which included the Thanksgiving order to the Berkeley Hundred. In the early 1900s, Lyon G. Tyler, a historian, was doing

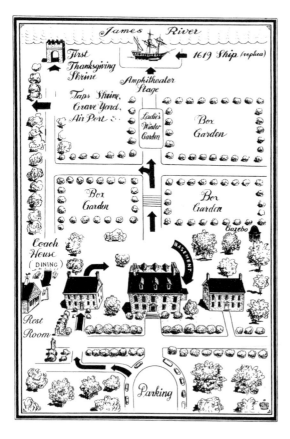

This diagram appears on the back of the ticket for admission to Berkeley Plantation in Virginia, the site of one of the claims for the "first" Thanksgiving. The location of the First Thanksgiving Shrine is noted at the top left side.

This drawing, "Coronado's March—Colorado," was created by Frederic Remington in 1890, hundreds of years after Coronado's expeditions through the Southwest. A famous artist, Remington was noted for the authentic details in his paintings. The man leading the burro is a padre, perhaps Fray Juan de Padilla.

research at the NYPL and stumbled upon the Thanksgiving order and publicized it. In the 1960s, a group of people formed a foundation, the Virginia First Thanksgiving Festival, to assert the 1619 claim as the first official Thanksgiving in America. Since 1970, they have held annual reenactments and a festival on the first Sunday in November.

What about the basis for the nine remaining claims? There are records and firsthand accounts of Coronado's expedition; an account of the 1564 French colony was written by René de Laudonnière, who escaped the massacre; a member of the Popham colony wrote a diary; members of the Jamestown Colony wrote letters and other accounts about the 1610 incident; the 1620 and 1623 events in Massachusetts are based on the journal of William Bradford, the governor of Plymouth Colony for thirty

This engraving depicts the stone column erected by French explorer Jean Ribault in 1562 on a bluff overlooking the St. John's River. Ribault claimed all the lands visible from the bluff for France. The official seal of King Charles IX is on the column. In 1564, René de Laudonnière established the French settlement of La Caroline, the site of one of the claims for the "first Thanksgiving." The engraving is titled *René de Laudonnière and the Indian Chief Athore Visit Ribault's Column*. It was engraved by Théodore de Bry, based on a painting by Jacques Le Moyne de Morgues, an artist who accompanied the 1564 expedition but left before the French settlers were killed by the Spanish.

years; the 1630 and 1631 events are based on accounts by John Winthrop, governor of the Massachusetts Bay Colony.

As for the familiar 1621 "Pilgrim and Indian" event, here is the story as I now understand it.

## Plymouth Colony

Many of the English colonists who established Plymouth Colony were Separatists who were seeking a place to freely practice their religion. (The label "Pilgrims" began to be applied to these colonists in the early 1800s.) They arrived on the *Mayflower* in November of 1620. In December they started building their settlement on the site of an abandoned village in the middle of the homeland of the Wampanoag people. Several years earlier, a plague had killed the inhabitants of the village, known as Patuxet to the Wampanoag.

Separatists did not celebrate Christmas or Easter. They rejected religious authorities such as the pope and religious symbols such as crosses and stained glass windows. In the Separatists' worldview, God controlled everything—good or bad—that happened. In order to maintain a proper relationship with God, the Separatists observed the weekly Sabbath on Sunday. In particularly bad times, such as a drought or epidemic, they held a Day of Humiliation and Fasting. In particularly good times, such as the end of a drought or epidemic or after a military victory, they observed a Day of Thanksgiving and Praise. Both of those types of days were marked by long religious services and prayers.

In the spring, Tisquantum, also known as Squanto, had shown the English colonists how to grow crops, including maize, the

[RIGHT] This statue of William Bradford is in Plymouth Rock State Park, Plymouth, Massachusetts.

[FAR RIGHT] A statue of Massasoit stands on Cole's Hill, Plymouth, Massachusetts.

multicolored corn with hard kernels that the English called Indian corn. In the fall, after the crops had been harvested, Governor William Bradford decided that the colonists should "rejoice together." They celebrated with food and games for almost a week. During that time, for three days, they were joined by many Wampanoag, including about ninety Wampanoag men and their *sachem*, or leader, Massasoit. They ate venison, duck, geese, and perhaps wild turkey. Other foods were probably cod, eel, shellfish, squash, and puddings made from corn, nuts, and dried berries. The colonists demonstrated their skills in marching in formation and shooting. Together, the Wampanoag and colonists played games, including competitive sports. Most likely there was also singing, music making, and perhaps dancing.

Edward Winslow, a Separatist, described the event in a letter he wrote to a friend in England. This letter is the basis for what later became widely known as the first Thanksgiving. In modern spelling, here is what Winslow wrote:

These street signs are in Weymouth, Massachusetts, a town about twenty miles north of Plymouth.

> Our harvest being gotten in, our governor sent four men on fowling, that so we might after a special manner rejoice together, after we had gathered the fruits of our labors; they four in one day killed as much fowl, as with a little help beside, served the Company almost a week, at which time, amongst other Recreations, we exercised our Arms, many of the Indians coming amongst us, and amongst the rest their greatest king Massasoit, with some ninety men, whom for three days we entertained and feasted, and they went out and killed five Deer, which they brought to the Plantation and bestowed on our Governor, and upon the Captain and others. And although it be not always so plentiful, as it was at this time with us, yet by the goodness of God, we are so far from want, that we often wish you partakers of our plenty.

After all my research into the various claims, I still favored the 1621 event with the English colonists and Wampanoag as the first Thanksgiving, perhaps in part because of my heritage—my father was from New England. But more than that, because the 1621 event was more like the Thanksgiving that we celebrate today. In

In the early 1900s, the artist Jean Louis Gerome Ferris created this painting, *First Thanksgiving,* of the 1621 event with the Pilgrims and Indians in Plymouth.

1621, the colonists and the Wampanoag came together in a secular gathering. They had a huge feast and played games, including competitive sports.

But as I continued doing more research, I realized that, in fact, none of these claims led directly to the establishment of Thanksgiving as a national holiday in the United States. That is not to say that they did not leave a mark on our historical memory. They did. However, the early claims are not the direct antecedents of the Thanksgiving that we celebrate today.

So what are the origins of the Thanksgiving that we celebrate today? What is the true story?

# ORIGINS OF OUR THANKSGIVING:
## Two Very Old Traditions

The true story of our modern Thanksgiving starts with two very old traditions: celebrating harvest festivals and proclaiming days of thanksgiving for special events.

### Harvest Festivals

People in all times and places have held harvest festivals. For most of human history, a good harvest meant the difference between life and death. (This is still true for parts of the world today.) During their spring harvest, the ancient Egyptians held a festival in honor of Min, their god of vegetation and fertility. In honor of Demeter, the goddess of agriculture, the ancient Greeks held a harvest festival in the fall. The ancient Romans held a harvest festival in October called Cerelia, after the goddess of grain. In the Old Testament, Moses directs the Israelites to celebrate the Feast of the Tabernacles, also called Sukkoth, after the harvest was gathered. Today Jews still observe Sukkoth in the fall. An ancient harvest festival called Homowo, a word that means "hooting at hunger," is still celebrated by the Ga people in Ghana. The ancient Korean harvest festival, Chusok, is also still celebrated in

The Fort Lee, New Jersey, high school marching band, dressed in traditional Korean clothing, plays at the 2006 celebration of Chusok, the Korean harvest festival, in Bergen County, New Jersey.

many places. In fact, while I was writing this book, I attended the Fifth Annual Chusok Festival of Bergen County, New Jersey, held in a park near my house.

Long before European colonists arrived in America, many Native American tribes, including the Wampanoag, celebrated harvest festivals throughout the year. Today the Wampanoag celebrate the harvest of the first wild berries in early spring, the Green Bean Harvest and Green Corn Harvest in midsummer, and the Cranberry Harvest in the fall. All the people join together to offer prayers of thanks to the Creator for providing food and to

In preparation for Sukkoth, many Jewish families erect a structure called a sukkah, where they gather in the evening to pray and eat. I live in an area where sukkahs are made of different materials such as canvas, wood, or nylon.

sing and dance and eat. These harvest festivals are part of the Wampanoags' practice of giving thanks every day. "Every day [is] a day of thanksgiving," says Gladys Widdiss, a contemporary tribal elder. "[We] give thanks to the dawn of the new day, at the end of the day, to the sun, to the moon. . . . There [is] always something to be thankful for."

In England, the homeland of the English settlers who came to Plymouth, the very old harvest festival was called harvest home, a time for feasting, singing and dancing, and merrymaking. Harvest

Since 1986, the Homowo African Arts & Cultures organization has held a monthlong Homowo Festival, a Ghanaian harvest celebration of welcoming and thanksgiving, in Portland, Oregon.

home was celebrated when the last sheaf of grain was harvested from the field and brought home, or stored for the winter. Different traditions were followed in various villages. In some, a figure called a corn dolly was made from the last sheaf of whatever grain—wheat, oats, rye, barley—had been harvested. In other villages, the Queen of the Harvest, a young girl dressed in white, and a crowd of people carrying ribbons and flowers accompanied the cart carrying the last harvest. The people who cut and gathered the grain, who were called reapers, and other field-workers followed the loaded cart and sang:

> Harvest home, harvest home
> We have plowed and we have sowed
> We have reaped, we have mowed

We have brought home every load

Hip, hip, hip, harvest home!

The Old World harvest festival traditions were established in the New World by various groups of settlers. People from Germany transplanted their harvest festival, Erntedanktag, to Pennsylvania. Dutch settlers in New Netherland, the area that stretched along the East Coast from New York to Delaware, celebrated harvest festivals there. Immigrants from England celebrated harvest home festivals wherever they settled throughout the colonies.

## Days of Thanksgiving for Special Events

The true story of our Thanksgiving is also connected to the very old tradition of both religious and civil authorities proclaiming days of thanksgiving

An illustration by Norman Borchardt in Konrad Bercovici's nonfiction book *On New Shores,* about the lives of immigrant groups in America in the 1920s. Bercovici "joined a harvest festival of Italians" near Ventura, California, on the road between Los Angeles and San Diego. He describes the road as decorated with Italian and American flags, the floats and musicians, and the carts loaded with "huge bunches of grapes, immense cabbages, giant artichokes . . . huge baskets of eggs and even goats, white and long-haired."

for special events—the end of a drought or an epidemic, the cessation of earthquakes, a military victory, a peace treaty, or safe arrival after a dangerous journey. Emperor Constantine declared days of thanksgiving when he established Constantinople in 330. In 1356, the Archbishop of Canterbury proclaimed eight days of thanksgiving to mark an important military victory won by the Black Prince (Edward of Woodstock, son of the English king Edward III). The English also celebrated a day of thanksgiving on November 5, 1605, the day after Guy Fawkes was caught and his plot to blow up the Houses of Parliament was foiled. The Dutch marked winning their independence from Spain in 1648 with days of thanksgiving.

The English colonists brought this tradition of giving thanks with them, and both religious and civil leaders regularly proclaimed days of thanksgiving for special events. Such special days would continue to be proclaimed until the mid-1800s in America.

## An Annual Day of General Thanksgiving

By the 1640s, a new type of thanksgiving proclamation emerged in the Connecticut River Valley farming towns of Wethersfield, Windsor, and Hartford. Civil leaders began to proclaim an annual day of general thanksgiving in the fall, whether or not there was a special event. On this day, people were to give thanks for the blessings of the past year and for the "fruits of the earth," or the harvest, thus bringing together both of these very old traditions—harvest festivals and days of thanksgiving.

Slowly this new tradition of proclaiming an annual day of general thanksgiving spread in the New England colonies, but not

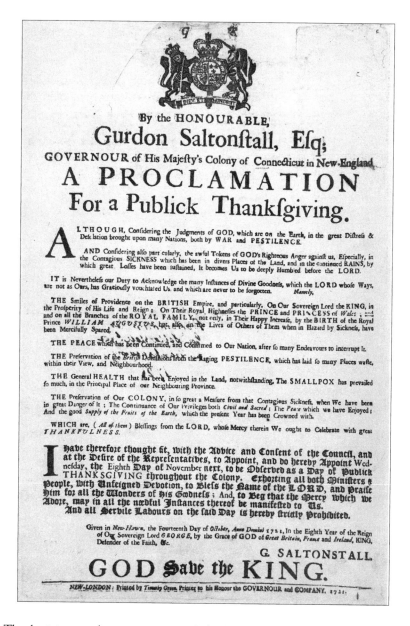

Thanksgiving proclamations were read aloud in town meetings and by ministers during church services. This proclamation was issued by Gurdon Saltonstall, the governor of the colony of Connecticut, for a "Publick Thanksgiving" to be held on Wednesday, November 8, 1721. In the proclamation, Saltonstall lists the "Judgments of GOD . . . WAR and PESTILENCE," but he also notes the "many instances of Divine Goodness," including the health of the king and his family, peace in the colonies, and the "good *Supply of the Fruits of the Earth*."

HARPER'S WEEKLY

JOURNAL OF CIVILIZATION

Vol. XLIII.—No. 2241
Copyright, 1899, by HARPER & BROTHERS
All Rights Reserved

NEW YORK, SATURDAY, DECEMBER 2, 1899

TEN CENTS A COPY
FOUR DOLLARS A YEAR

THANKSGIVING IN THE OLDEN TIME.
BELLMAN READING THE GOVERNOR'S PROCLAMATION IN A NEW ENGLAND TOWN.—DRAWN BY STANLEY M. ARTHUR.

*Thanksgiving in the Olden Time: Bellman Reading the Governor's Proclamation in a New England Town,* by Stanley M. Arthur, was on the cover of *Harper's Weekly,* December 2, 1899.

without some resistance. In the Massachusetts Bay Colony, ministers and other leaders debated whether or not people might start taking God's blessings for granted if days of thanksgiving were not linked to special events. The debate, however, was drowned out by the growing popular demand for an annual, general Thanksgiving Day. People liked the idea of gathering their family together, attending a church service to give thanks, and celebrating the annual harvest with a feast.

By the early 1700s, annual Thanksgiving Days had been proclaimed by the governors of Connecticut, Massachusetts, and New Hampshire, although not on any regular date. The emergence of this new tradition in the New England colonies did not, however, end the very old tradition of proclaiming days of thanksgiving for special events.

## Juliana Smith's New England Thanksgiving Dinner

Three years after the start of the Revolutionary War in 1776, Juliana Smith, a girl who lived in Massachusetts, described her family's Thanksgiving Day dinner in a letter she wrote to her cousin Betsey Smith:

> This year it was Uncle Simeon's turn to have the
> dinner at his house, but of course we all helped
> them as they help us when it is our turn, & there
> is always enough for us all to do. All the baking of
> pies & cakes was done at our house & we had the
> big oven heated & filled twice each day for three
> days before it was all done, & *everything was GOOD*.

Juliana reported that because of the war they could not buy raisins for the pies, "but our good red cheries dried without the pits, did almost as well & happily Uncle Simeon still had some spices in store." According to Juliana, the servants set up two large tables to accommodate about forty people—her uncles and aunts and cousins and five orphans and four "Old Ladies who have no longer Homes or Children of their own" and "our Two Grandmothers." The grandmothers, Juliana wrote, "are always handsome old Ladies, but now, many thought, they were handsomer than ever, & happy they were to look around upon so many of their descendants." The new neighbors, who had moved from New York, were there too. "They had never seen a Thanksgiving Dinner before," Juliana wrote, "having been used to keep Christmas Day instead."

There was no roast beef on the menu: "It all must go to the Army, & too little they get, poor fellows," Juliana wrote. Instead they ate venison in addition to their usual Thanksgiving foods—roast pork, roast turkey, goose, pigeon pasties, and "an abundance of good Vegetables." Their desserts included mince pies, pumpkin pies, apple tarts, and Indian pudding. It was a cold day, and they were glad to have a fire in the dining hall, Juliana reported. "But," she continued, "by the time the dinner was one-half over those of us who were on the fire side of one Table were forced to get up & carry our plates with us around to the far side of the other Table, while those who had sat there were as glad to bring their plates around to the fire side to get warm."

Juliana described how Uncle Simeon "kept both Tables in a roar of laughter" with his stories and how he and her father and her uncle Paul sang hymns and ballads. "You know how fine their voices go together," she wrote. "Then we all sang a Hymn and afterwards my dear Father led us in prayers, remembering all Absent Friends." After dinner, they sat around the fire "as close as we could, & cracked nuts, & sang songs. . . . *You know nobody* can exceed the two Grandmothers at telling tales of all the things they have seen."

Juliana's brother Jack, who was a college student, arrived after riding his horse for several days through deep snow. He brought an orange for each of the grandmothers, Juliana reported. "But Alas! They were frozen in his saddle bags. We soaked the frost out in cold water, but I guess they weren't as good as they should have been."

## A National Thanksgiving Day

During the American Revolution, the Continental Congress adopted the New England tradition of proclaiming both an annual, general Thanksgiving Day and days of thanksgiving for special events.

The first day of thanksgiving for a special event was proclaimed for December 18, 1777, to mark the defeat of the British army at Saratoga. The first annual, general Thanksgiving Proclamation was passed in 1778 and each year thereafter until 1784, the year the Revolutionary War officially ended with the signing of the Treaty of Paris.

The tradition of proclaiming a special day of thanksgiving resumed in 1789. It was initiated by Representative Elias Boudinot, of New Jersey, who proposed that Congress ask President

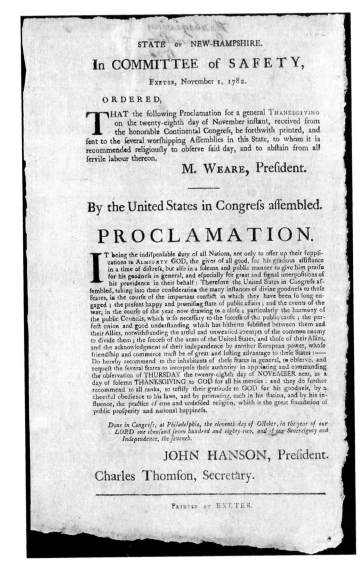

This document was issued in 1782. The bottom part is a proclamation by
the "United States in Congress," or the Continental Congress, for the
observation of Thursday, November 28, as a "day of solemn Thanksgiving to
God for all his mercies." The top part is a recommendation to observe the day
by the Committee of Safety in New Hampshire, a group formed in each state,
except Georgia, to support the Revolutionary War. At this time in history, the
Continental Congress only had the authority to recommend that states
designate a day for thanksgiving; it was up to the governor to make the final
decision. This would also be true for presidents of the United States, until
Congress passed a law making Thanksgiving Day a legal holiday.

Washington to proclaim a day of thanksgiving to mark the adoption of the United States Constitution.

But not everyone was happy with the Constitution. A group called the Antifederalists thought that the Constitution created a central government that was too powerful and would overrun the rights of states and of individuals. A representative from South Carolina, Thomas Tucker, denounced Boudinot's proposal:

> Why should the President direct the people to do what perhaps they have no mind to do? They may not be inclined to return thanks for a Constitution until they have experienced that it promotes their safety and happiness. . . . If a day of Thanksgiving must take place, let it be done by the authority of the several States. They know best what reason their constituents have to be pleased with the establishment of the Constitution.

In the end, Boudinot's proposal passed and President Washington issued a Thanksgiving Day Proclamation for November 26, 1789, to "be devoted by the People of these States to the service of that great and glorious Being, who is the beneficent Author of all the good that was, that is, or that will be—That we may then unite in rendering him our sincere and humble thanks . . . for the peaceable and rational manner in which we have been enabled to establish constitutions of government for our safety and happiness . . . particularly the national One now lately instituted."

Washington issued his second Thanksgiving Day Proclamation for February 19, 1795: "I, George Washington, President of the

United States, do recommend to all religious societies and denominations, and to all persons whomsoever, within the United States to set apart and observe . . . a day of public thanksgiving and prayer." Washington's successor, John Adams, issued two proclamations for "a day of solemn humiliation, fasting, and prayer . . . accompanied by fervent thanksgiving," one to be held in May, the other in April. But the next president, Thomas Jefferson, refused. Jefferson firmly believed that the president had no authority to "direct the religious exercises of his constituents."

President James Madison issued two "day of thanksgiving" proclamations to mark the end of the War of 1812—one to be held in January, the other in April. Then that was it. Forty-eight years would pass before another president proclaimed a national Thanksgiving Day.

How that happened is another piece of the true story of our Thanksgiving. And that piece involves a determined woman, a proper Victorian woman, the mother of five children and arguably one of the most powerful magazine editors in American history— Sarah Josepha Hale.

# THREE

# SARAH JOSEPHA HALE'S CAMPAIGN: "Day of National Thanksgiving"

"We children had to trot to keep up with her." That is how Sarah Hale Hunter remembered her grandmother, Sarah Josepha Hale. Hunter also recalled how Hale enlisted her grandchildren to search for pins that dropped on the floor. The prize for finding three pins was five raisins. "I never was able to figure out the logic of *five* raisins as a reward for *three* pins, unless it was grandmother's generosity. She loved to give."

## Her Appearance and Accomplishments

Sarah Josepha Hale had a smile "which, though it broke slowly, ended in a flash." She parted her brown hair in the middle and fashioned it in side curls that cascaded down her face (a style of the 1820s that she never changed). She was of medium height, and her posture was erect. Her forehead was broad, and her feet and hands were small. She kept her own concoction of hand lotion—lard, rosewater, and coconut milk—in her desk drawer and used it every time she washed her hands. At night Sarah Hale dipped little strips of heavy brown paper in fresh apple vinegar and laid them on her temples to prevent "crow's feet," or wrinkles, from forming beside her hazel eyes.

Sarah Josepha
Hale, painted by
W. B. Chambers
and engraved for
*Godey's Lady's Book*
by W. G.
Armstrong.

During a time when fierce advocates for women's rights—Lucretia Mott, Lucy Stone, Amelia Bloomer, Elizabeth Cady Stanton, Susan B. Anthony—were raising their voices, Sarah Hale kept her voice carefully modulated. She appeared to be very conventional—she wore bustles and crinolines, and she embraced the idea that there were separate spheres for men and women. But in spite of, or perhaps because of, her traditional ways, Sarah Josepha Hale was an extraordinarily influential magazine editor for much of the nineteenth century. She relentlessly pushed for educational opportunities for girls and women. She wrote editorials insisting that women be admitted to medical school. She supported women writers by publishing their work, including Harriet Beecher Stowe's first stories.

In a biography of Hale published in 1931, the author Ruth E. Finley begins chapter one with a list of Hale's accomplishments. Here are just a few:

- She was responsible for Thanksgiving as a national holiday. . . .
- She was the first to advocate women as teachers in public schools. . . .

- She started the first day nursery—boon to working mothers. . . .
- She was the first to suggest public playgrounds. . . .
- She was among the earliest to recognize health and sanitation as civic problems and the first to crusade for remedial measures. . . .
- She raised the money that finished Bunker Hill Monument. . . .
- She was the author of some two dozen books and hundreds of poems, including the best known children's rhyme . . . "Mary Had a Little Lamb."

## Born a New Englander

Sarah Josepha Hale was born Sarah Josepha Buell on October 24, 1788, in Newport, New Hampshire. Because she was a girl, Sarah did not have opportunities to go to school. "I was mainly educated by my mother," she later recalled. "The books to which I had access were few . . . but they were such as required to be studied—and I did study them. Next to the Bible and *The Pilgrim's Progress*, my earliest reading was Milton, Addison, Pope, Johnson, Cowper, Burns, and a portion of Shakespeare." She also learned from her brother, Horatio, who taught her what he learned at school, including when he went to college. "To my brother Horatio, I owe what knowledge I have of Latin, of the higher branches of mathematics, and of mental philosophy," she wrote. "He often regretted that I could not, like himself, have the privilege of a college education."

SARAH JOSEPHA BUELL HALE
——— 1788-1879 ———
Prominent humanitarian, poet and
author was born and taught school
in Guild section of Newport. Wid-
owed mother of five, she edited
"Godey's Lady's Book", 1837-1877;
composed poem now called "Mary
Had A Little Lamb"; advocated
proclamation of Thanksgiving Day
as national festival; and appealed
constantly for higher education
for women.

Historic marker in the Guild section of Newport, New Hampshire.

At the age of eighteen, Sarah started teaching school. At twenty-five, she married David Hale, a popular young lawyer who had recently moved to Newport. He too shared his learning with Sarah. From eight o'clock until ten o'clock at night, they read and studied together—French, botany, mineralogy, geology, and other subjects. "How I enjoyed those hours!" she recalled.

Sarah Hale was pregnant with their third child when the doctor said she had "quick consumption," or tuberculosis, and that she would not survive the pregnancy.

Sarah's grandchildren loved to hear her tell the story of what happened after the doctor made his diagnosis:

> One evening David—your grandfather—had been reading aloud to me as I reclined on the sofa, when right in the middle of a sentence he suddenly closed the book and walked out of the house without a word. He was gone a long time.

Where he went or what he did he never told me.
But when he came back he picked me up in his
arms.

    "Listen," he said, "you are not going to die. I
won't *let* you!"

The next morning David arranged to leave their children with
a relative, and he took Sarah on a carriage trip through the
mountains. They traveled for six weeks. "It was beautiful weather;
and I ate grapes," Sarah recalled. "We had heard of the grape
cure. . . . Also . . . that fresh air ought to be good for sick lungs. I
remember we stopped at the doctor's house on the way out of
town, and he vowed David would never bring me home alive. But
David did bring me home, cured."

## Turned to Writing

Four years later, David died of pneumonia. Sarah gave birth to
their fifth child two weeks after that. "I was left poor," Sarah Hale
later said. The year was 1822, and there were few ways that
women could earn a living. She tried sewing, then she turned to
writing. In 1827 her first novel, *Northwood,* was published. The first
book written by a man or woman that dealt with slavery, *Northwood* also presented a realistic and accurate record of life in
postcolonial America. Because of the success of her book, Sarah
Josepha Hale was asked to become the editor of *Ladies' Magazine,* a
new magazine for women readers that she soon renamed *American
Ladies' Magazine* to reflect her intent to publish American writers,
including women. She was forty years old.

*Northwood* not only launched Hale on her career as an editor but also reflected her passion for Thanksgiving Day. She wrote a lengthy dialogue between Squire Romilly (the father of the book's hero, Sidney Romilly) and Mr. Frankford (an Englishman and friend of Sidney's) about the origin (the 1631 event) and purpose of Thanksgiving—the belief that Americans "derive our privileges and blessing" from God. She also foreshadowed the crusade that she later launched:

> "Is Thanksgiving Day universally observed in America?" inquired Mr. Frankford.
>
> "Not yet; but I trust it will become so. We have too few holidays. Thanksgiving, like the Fourth of July, should be considered a national festival, and observed by all our people."

Hale devoted two chapters in her book to Thanksgiving, "A Thanksgiving Sermon" and "Thanksgiving Dinner." The people in the congregation who heard the minister's sermon were, according to Hale's description, attentive: "No eye was closed . . . nor was a nod, or even a look or action, expressive of weariness, seen throughout the assembly." As for the dinner, Hale described every detail, from the color of the woodwork in the parlor to the damask cloth covering the long table. The menu was extraordinary: "The roasted turkey took precedence on this occasion, being placed at the head of the table . . . sending forth the rich odor of savory stuffing. . . . A sirloin of beef, flanked on either side by a leg of pork and loin of mutton . . . innumerable bowls of gravy and plates of vegetables. . . . A goose and a pair of ducklings . . . a chicken pie. . . . Plates of pickles, preserves and butter. . . . A huge plum pudding, custards and pies of every name and description ever known in Yankee land . . . rich cake, and a variety of sweetmeats and fruits."

## Sarah Josepha Hale's Campaign

In 1837, Sarah Josepha Hale became the editor of what would become *Godey's Lady's Book.* Under her guidance, it grew to have a circulation of 150,000 readers, an astonishing number at that time. She later used the pages of the magazine to advocate for her campaign to ensure that: "THE LAST THURSDAY IN NOVEMBER

In the mid-1800s, articles and illustrations about Thanksgiving appear in the November issues of popular magazines. *Thanksgiving Day—The Dinner* was in the November 27, 1858, issue of the widely read magazine *Harper's Weekly.*

shall be the DAY OF NATIONAL THANKSGIVING for the American people."

She selected the last Thursday in November for several reasons: "Because then the agricultural labors of the year are generally completed; the elections are over; those autumnal diseases which usually prevail more or less at the South have ceased, and the summer wanderers are gathered to their homes." "Thursday," Hale wrote, "is the most convenient day of the week for a domestic holiday." She also pointed out that George Washington selected a Thursday in his Thanksgiving Proclamation.

Year after year, Sarah Josepha Hale persisted in the "habit of urging on the attention of our readers and friends . . . the plan of a National Thanksgiving." Every year, she wrote a special editorial on the subject. She wrote thousands of letters to governors of states, territories, and military commanders, to ambassadors and five different presidents. She called upon the rest of the press to join in supporting her efforts.

## Much to Offer

Why was Sarah Josepha Hale so passionate about Thanksgiving? Undoubtedly she was influenced by growing up in New England where an annual autumn Thanksgiving Day was already well established. For her, it was a special time for families to attend church together and share a feast. She was also responding to the dramatic transformation of the United States.

Between 1790 and 1850, new modes of transportation were developed: steamboats and then railroads. Mills and factories were built. Large cities grew: New York City's population

A copy of the November 1865 issue of *Godey's Lady's Book* in the Sarah Josepha Hale Room, Richards Free Library, Newport, New Hampshire.

As part of her campaign, Sarah Josepha Hale wrote scores of letters to the governors of the states and territories. Massachusetts governor Nathaniel P. Banks sent her this response, dated September 28, 1863: "It will afford me very great pleasure to comply with your request and make the appointment for Thanksgiving on the 24th, the last Thursday of November. The Governors of Rhode Island and New Hampshire will do the same."

exploded from 33,000 to 515,000. People were on the move and families were spreading apart. Between 1790 and 1820, 800,000 people had left New England and settled in Michigan, Iowa, Wisconsin, Indiana, and Illinois. Hale herself moved to Philadelphia, Pennsylvania, in 1841. Her son William spent years in Galveston, Texas. In the 1840s, a mass of new immigrants poured into the country. Then there was the issue of slavery, which was becoming increasingly contentious and divisive.

In such tumultuous times, Hale believed that a national Thanksgiving Day had much to offer America. Her vision was of all Americans "uniting as one Great Family Republic." She believed that celebrating a national Thanksgiving Day would "awaken in American hearts the love of home and country, of thankfulness to God, and peace between brethren."

In one of her editorials, Hale pointed out that Americans had only two national holidays to celebrate: Washington's birthday in February and the Fourth of July. "These are patriotic and political," she wrote.

> Are not the sounds of war borne on the breezes of
> those festivals? One comes in the cold of winter;
> the other in the heat of summer; while the
> glorious autumn of the year, when blessings are
> gathered in, has no day of remembrance for her
> gifts of peace. Should not the women of America
> have one festival in whose rejoicings they can
> fully participate?

## Americans Celebrate

Hale kept track of where and when Americans celebrated a national Thanksgiving Day. Her list included states and territories; American ships in various ports; and American missionaries, students, and diplomats in foreign countries.

"Last year," she wrote in her 1852 editorial, "twenty nine States, and all the Territories, united in the festival. This year, we trust that Virginia and Vermont will come into this arrangement. . . . Henceforth wherever an American is found, the last Thursday in November would be the Thanksgiving Day . . . [and] every heart would on one day in each year, beat in unison of enjoyment and thankfulness." In a later editorial, she noted that Thanksgiving dinners were held in "London, Paris, Liverpool, Frankfort, Berlin, Florence, and Rome . . . in Japan at the mouth of the Amoor River, in St. Petersburg and in Rio de Janeiro."

Many of these celebrations were initiated by transplanted New Englanders and other settlers who cherished the holiday.

The governor of Oregon succumbed to the pressure of seventy-six Oregon City women. "Be it known that in conformity with the wishes of many citizens of Oregon," he wrote, "I appoint and set apart Thursday, the 29th of December, 1859, as a day to be kept for PUBLIC THANKSGIVING." The governor of the Minnesota Territory appeared to need a hint from someone, according to an account by Mrs. Isaac Atwater: "November passed and week by week New Englanders looked for the announcement of their ancient and beloved festival, but even the sacred last Thursday went by without it, and dismay and homesickness filled all hearts. Our good governor must have been of Scotch or Dutch pedigree to have over-looked a duty of such importance; but at last a hint was given him, a brief proclamation was forthcoming, and the day duly celebrated."

A transplanted New Englander who lived in Louisiana observed the first Thanksgiving there on January 15, 1846. "Thanks to His excellency Governor Mouton!" the New Englander wrote to relatives in Indiana, "He has seen the evil of his ways, and has at length repented and announced that *this year* and *ever after* the people of Louisiana must celebrate a day of Thanksgiving. . . . We are going to try to have a *real* Yankee dinner, pumpkin pies and everything to match."

## The Opposition

The idea that Thanksgiving was a New England tradition was one of the reasons people who were not native New Englanders were slow in adopting it. By the late 1880s, however, a widely read newspaper reported, "Each year Thanksgiving becomes more and more a national and less a New-England holiday." Other people felt that a thanksgiving day should be proclaimed only for special events. Then there were people who resisted the idea of a national Thanksgiving. They thought it should be up to each state to decide the if and when of having an annual thanksgiving day. But these sentiments had little effect on the growing numbers of people who heeded Sarah Josepha Hale's advice and gathered together to celebrate Thanksgiving Day on the last Thursday in November. From 1849 to 1851, Frederika Bremer, a Swedish writer, traveled throughout America. "In America," she wrote, "there is annually celebrated what is called the Thanksgiving Festival.

It occurs in the autumn when the harvest is finished. The families then assemble to rejoice together, and to distribute the earth's best wealth amid praises of the giver."

### Sarah Josepha Hale and Abraham Lincoln

During the first two years of the Civil War, the leaders of the Union and the Confederacy—Abraham Lincoln and Jefferson Davis—declared special days of thanksgiving for military victories. Lincoln declared one on August 6, 1863, to mark the Union victories, including the Battle of Gettysburg. About that time, Sarah Josepha Hale may have met with Lincoln. Although there is no record of their meeting, Hale's grandson remembered his father saying that "his mother had visited President Lincoln and had found him a very kindly and interested gentleman."

On September 28, 1863, Sarah Josepha Hale wrote to President Lincoln. The purpose of her letter was to "Entreat President Lincoln to put forth his Proclamation, appointing the last Thursday in November . . . as the National Thanksgiving. . . . Thus by the noble example and action of the President of the United States, the permanency and unity of our Great American Festival of Thanksgiving would be forever secured." She enclosed copies of three of her editorials with her letter.

A few days later, on October 3, 1863, President Lincoln issued a Proclamation of Thanksgiving for the last Thursday of November. He called upon "my fellow citizens in every part of the United States, and also those who are at sea and those who are sojourning in foreign lands, to set apart and observe . . . a day of Thanksgiving and Praise."

The first paragraph of a letter that Sarah Josepha Hale wrote to President Abraham Lincoln reads: "Sir. Permit me, as Editress of the 'Lady's Book,' to request a few minutes of your precious time, while laying before you a subject of deep interest to myself and—as I trust—even to the President of our Republic, of some importance. This subject is to have the *day of our annual Thanksgiving made a National and fixed Union Festival.*"

Lincoln's proclamation was in the tradition of an annual, general Thanksgiving Day. Sarah Josepha Hale had realized her goal, part of it at least. For she knew that a presidential proclamation only applied to federal employees and residents of the District of Columbia. As for the rest of the country, a president could only recommend that governors proclaim Thanksgiving Day. It would take an act of Congress to have a national Thanksgiving become an official holiday, thus "forever secured," and not dependent on the whim of future presidents and governors.

This illustration, *Thanksgiving Day, November 24, 1864, United We Stand*, appeared in *Harper's Weekly*. Since the 1700s, Thanksgiving had been politicized—proclamations and sermons were used to advocate a particular cause or express a political position. Here, the famous political cartoonist Thomas Nast expressed a pro-Union perspective. At the center, Nast placed Abraham Lincoln, who had just been elected for a second term as president, shaking hands with General Ulysses Grant, commander of the Union troops. The female figure in the top left image symbolizes Maryland, and the caption reads "Thank God for Maryland Freeing Her Slaves"; the female figure in the top right image is the mythic Columbia (a feminized version of Columbus), a widely used symbol of America. The caption reads "Thank God for Our Union Victories"; the captions for the middle panels that depict men reading newspapers read, from left to right, "In Europe" and "In Rebeldom" (note the dejected expressions). The bottom middle panel with the Union generals reads "Blessed are the Peace-Makers." The two bottom side panels read, from left to right, "In the Field" (note the soldier kneeling on the ground and carving the turkey) and "On Board" (note the sailors serving Thanksgiving dinner to their shipmates).

## Final Appeal

Now, Sarah Josepha Hale focused her efforts on getting Congress to pass legislation making Thanksgiving the "third American holiday." She continued her efforts until 1877, when she retired at the age of eighty-nine, two years before her death.

"This is probably the last occasion upon which the Editress of the Lady's Book will speak to the public through the pages of this magazine, on a subject which has been near to her heart for many years," she wrote in her last editorial. "Let the Fifty-fifth Congress, in the name of the American people, enact that from henceforward the last Thursday in November shall be observed, throughout the length and breadth of our land, as the day of our National Thanksgiving."

Sixty-four years would pass before Congress established Thanksgiving as an official holiday. Nevertheless, the tradition of an annual national Thanksgiving Day was firmly established. For that, Sarah Josepha Hale was largely responsible. Perhaps, as some people have already claimed, she was the mother of our Thanksgiving.

## Sixty-four Years Later

Congress finally made Thanksgiving Day a legal holiday in 1941, in response to a conflict that erupted in 1939. That year, November had five Thursdays. Hoping that more shopping days after Thanksgiving would mean more sales, a national association of merchants asked President Franklin Delano Roosevelt (FDR) to change Thanksgiving from the last Thursday, the traditional day, to the fourth Thursday. They had made the same request in 1933, another year with five Thursdays, but FDR had refused. This time he agreed and made the announcement in August.

It is unlikely that FDR could have anticipated the controversy that erupted in response to his announcement. Telegrams and letters poured into the White House. How dare he change the "hallowed traditional" date! What would happen to all the traditional Thanksgiving Day football games? What about school vacation days that were already set? "I am afraid your change for Thanksgiving," wrote the owner of a calendar company, "is going to cause the calendar manufacturers untold grief." Politicians, ministers, newspaper editors, and cartoonists expressed their opinions on both sides. Some people kept a sense of humor, including Shelby O. Bennett of Shinnston, West Virginia, who wrote the following letter:

> Mr. President:
>
> I see by the paper this morning where you want to change Thanksgiving Day to November 23 of which I heartily approve. Thanks.
>
> Now, there are some things that I would like done and would appreciate your approval.
>
> 1. Have Sunday changed to Wednesday;
> 2. Have Mondays to be Christmas;
> 3. Have it strictly against the Will of God to work on Tuesday;
> 4. Have Thursday to be Pay Day with time and one-half for overtime;
> 5. Require everyone to take Friday and Saturday off for a fishing trip down the Potomac.

# H. J. RES. 41

---

# JOINT RESOLUTION

Making the last Thursday in November a legal holiday.

1     *Resolved by the Senate and House of Representatives*

2   *of the United States of America in Congress assembled,*

3   That the last Thursday of November in each year after the

4   year 1941 be known as Thanksgiving Day, and is hereby

5   made a legal public holiday to all intents and purposes and

6   in the same manner as the 1st day of January, the 22d day

7   of February, the 30th day of May, the 4th day of July, the

8   first Monday of September, the 11th day of November, and

9   Christmas Day are now made by law public holidays.

    Passed the House of Representatives October 6, 1941.

    Attest:

*Clerk.*

The confusion over which Thursday should be designated for Thanksgiving Day continued as the United States Congress tried to resolve the matter. The first bill, passed on October 6, 1941, set the "last Thursday of November."

In the Senate of the United States,

*December 9, 1941.*

*Resolved,* That the joint resolution from the House of Representatives (H. J. Res. 41) entitled "Joint Resolution making the last Thursday in November a legal holiday", do pass with the following

## AMENDMENTS:

Line 3, strike out [last] and insert: *fourth*

Amend the title so as to read: "Joint resolution making the fourth Thursday in November a legal holiday."

Attest:

*Secretary.*

Two months later that bill was amended to change it to the "fourth Thursday in November."

With these in view and hoping you will give me some consideration at your next Congress.

Yours very truly,

Shelby O. Bennett

Twenty-one states changed the date. Sixteen states refused. Thus, 1939 became known as the year of two Thanksgivings.

All that uproar and confusion prompted Congress to finally make Thanksgiving a legal holiday and to set a fixed date. The

House of Representatives passed a resolution declaring the last Thursday in November to be the legal Thanksgiving Day. The Senate amended that resolution to set the date as the fourth Thursday, in order to accommodate the years when November has five Thursdays. The House agreed, ending the confusion and establishing Thanksgiving as a national holiday.

**The True Story**

As you can see, the origins of the Thanksgiving that we celebrate today cannot be directly traced to the inspiration of a single historical event, such as the 1621 Pilgrim and Indian feast. Its origins are much more complicated. The true story involves multiple influences—two very old traditions and the activism of a determined woman—that were finally officially recognized by an act of Congress.

But what about the "Pilgrim and Indian" story that we all know so well?

# FOUR

# THE "PILGRIM AND INDIAN" STORY

All of the teens and a majority of the adults who answered my survey believed that the Pilgrims and Indians celebrated the first Thanksgiving in Plymouth in 1621. Joyce Ruggieri was one of the minority of adults who doubted that. "Thanksgiving did not happen as it was portrayed," she wrote on my survey. Another doubter wrote, "The first Thanksgiving was probably more complicated than the simplistic version we learned about as children." I, on the other hand, was with the majority who believed that the "Pilgrim and Indian" story was synonymous with the Thanksgiving holiday.

However, as I delved more deeply into this topic, I was surprised to discover that the "Pilgrim and Indian" story was *not* the inspiration for the establishment of the national Thanksgiving Day in the 1800s. That the spread of Thanksgiving was *not* about commemorating the 1621 event.

## A Research Quest

Discovering that led me on a research quest to answer the question: *When* did the "Pilgrim and Indian" story become associated with the Thanksgiving holiday?

This is one of the first illustrations, *Thanksgiving Week—1621*, that was based on Edward Winslow's firsthand account of the 1621 event. In the article that accompanied the illustration, the artist Charles Stanley Reinhart explained the "subject of my picture" and quoted from Winslow's letter to his friend in England. The illustration and article appeared in *Harper's Weekly*, dated December 1, 1894.

I found the answer to that question by reading everything Sarah Josepha Hale wrote about Thanksgiving, a variety of other publications, and a collection of magazines and history books for children. Here is what I learned.

## Sarah Josepha Hale

Hale never wrote about the "Pilgrim and Indian" Thanksgiving story. In her novel *Northwood*, a character explained that Thanksgiving originated with the 1631 event in Boston, when a day of thanksgiving was proclaimed after the ship arrived and saved the colonists from starvation. In two of her editorials, she connected Thanksgiving to the Jewish tradition of the "Feast of the Weeks" (also called Shavuot) and to the traditional "ingathering" of the harvest. In one editorial, she wrote, "To the Colony of Massachusetts belongs the honor of introducing this holiday, soon after the settlement of Boston [it was settled in 1630]. . . . From that Colony the observance of Thanksgiving became the custom in all New England, then advanced slowly but steadily on to the Middle States and the West."

## Other Publications

Newspaper articles throughout the 1800s and early 1900s agreed that Thanksgiving originated in New England; however, some cited the events in 1623 (when the rain ended the drought) or in 1631 (when the supply ship arrived). One newspaper article stated the date as 1623, but described the 1621 event. Accounts written during this time typically referred to the Indians as the "invited guests" of the Pilgrims, a common interpretation, even today—but one that is not supported by the only firsthand account of the event, Edward Winslow's letter.

Let's look again at what Winslow wrote about the arrival of Massasoit and his men: "Our harvest being gotten in . . . at which time amongst other Recreations, we exercised our Arms, many of the Indians coming amongst us, and amongst the rest their greatest king Massasoit, with some ninety men, whom for three days we entertained and feasted. . . ."

What do you think? Some historians suggest another interpretation: Massasoit and his men arrived after the English

The First Thanksgiving Dinner.

This picture by F. W. Read of the 1621 event is in the 1898 book for young readers *The Story of the Thirteen Colonies*, by H. A. Guerber.

colonists had been feasting and shooting off their muskets ("we exercised our Arms") to find out what the colonists were up to. After all, Massasoit and the English leaders had recently agreed to a peace treaty.

Winslow's letter was first published in 1622 in a book known as *Mourt's Relations*. More than two hundred years later, in 1841, Alexander Young rediscovered Winslow's letter and published it in a book titled *Chronicles of the Pilgrim Fathers of the Colony of Plymouth, 1602–1625*. Young included a footnote in which he labeled Winslow's description of the English colonists and Wampanoag feasting together as "the first thanksgiving." Young's claim does not appear to have had much influence in shaping the Thanksgiving story in the nineteenth century. However, by reprinting Winslow's letter and calling the event "the first thanksgiving," Young put out a story that could be picked up by people at a later time, as it eventually was.

## Children's Magazines and History Books

In the 1800s, many articles, stories, poems, and activities about Thanksgiving appeared in *The Youth's Companion.* But not one mentioned the "Pilgrim and Indian" Thanksgiving story. There were no stories about Thanksgiving in the children's history books that I examined, until the late 1890s. A brief mention that "the fast day was turned into a thanksgiving day" was in a book published in 1895. The first explicit account appeared in *The Story of the Thirteen Colonies* by H. A. Guerber, which was published in 1898. In a section titled "The First American Thanksgiving," Guerber conflated the 1621 event and the 1623 event. She referred to the Indians as "savages," described Massasoit as the "dirty chief," and ended with the inaccurate claim that "after this 'Thanksgiving Day,' as the Pilgrims named it, a feast like it was kept every year in New England." Although it is not possible to know how many people were influenced by Guerber's account, elements of her version were typically reflected in subsequent accounts of the first Thanksgiving.

## Centuries of Conflicts

The fact that the "Pilgrim and Indian" story was not the inspiration for the national Thanksgiving Day should not have surprised me.

Ever since the 1600s, warfare between Native Americans and the European settlers was all too common. In 1622, a raiding party of Native Americans killed all the colonists at Berkeley Plantation in

Plaque commemorating Metacomet (Metacom) attached to a rock at the top of the town square in Plymouth, Massachusetts.

Virginia. In 1636 and 1637, Puritan forces wiped out the Pequot, a victory that was celebrated by a special day of thanksgiving. In King Philip's War (1675–76), the New England colonists almost annihilated the Narragansetts, Nipmucks, and Wampanoag. Ironically, the Wampanoag had at first helped the English colonists survive and shared the feast in 1621. The war was named after Metacom, Massasoit's son, who was known as Philip and was the Wampanoag's tribal *sachem*, or leader. Metacom was killed and beheaded, and for more than twenty years, his head was displayed on the end of a pike in Plymouth.

Such conflicts continued through the 1700s. In 1763, Pontiac, an Ottawa chief, led a confederation of Hurons, Kickapoo,

Chippewas, and other tribes in an attempt to push the British out of the Great Lakes region. In 1782, American forces under George Rogers Clark defeated the Shawnee and Delaware Indians who lived in the Midwest.

In the 1800s, as the United States expanded its boundaries and settlers moved west, the conflict intensified. Then in the 1890s, the battles ended. The Native Americans were defeated; the ones who had survived were confined on reservations.

## No Threat

Within a few years, newspapers were carrying stories about the celebration of Thanksgiving Day on Indian reservations. On November 24, 1901, the *New York Times* printed an article titled "Thanksgiving on Indian Reservations." According to the article, "the Government authorities are willing that Thanksgiving Day shall become a festal time for the reservation wards of the Nation." As was common at that time, the article was replete with racist stereotypical language—"dusky redskins" and "squaws." The Indians are described as having "had to forsake the scalping knife for the plow" and reservations are described as places "where the Indians have had an opportunity to become thoroughly civilized."

The article concluded with a report from Chilocco, an Indian school run by the U.S. government where "some 600 young Indians" attended.

> Those who have parents are allowed a visit from
> them on that day. For several days prior to
> Thanksgiving the trails leading to Chilocco

School are lined with wagons loaded with Indians.
They camp on the Chilocco Reservation. The
students are allowed to go into camp with their
parents, but cannot spend the night with them,
for fear of evil effects. . . . The parents see the
glad faces of their children, neat-appearing boys
and girls . . . it seems for the best. For are not
their children happy . . . where they are being
advanced in the ways of the white people?

The fact that the Native Americans were no longer viewed as
a threat allowed for the emergence of the "Pilgrim and Indian"
Thanksgiving story. Another factor was that Plymouth Colony
had already become established as the "founding story" of the
United States. Every country has a story about when and how the
country began. This story can serve many purposes—to present
a particular view of history, to perpetuate certain values, to unite
people around a common belief, and to justify an established
social order.

During the 1800s, the voyage of the *Mayflower* and the Pilgrims'
(as they were now known) quest for religious freedom became
the founding story of the United States. This happened for
several reasons, including efforts to promote Plymouth that
began in 1820 with a big celebration to commemorate the bicen-
tennial of the landing of the Pilgrims. Daniel Webster, a leg-
endary orator, gave a speech in which he extolled the "labors" and
"virtues" and "piety" of the "Pilgrim Fathers." Webster's speech
became known as the "Plymouth Oration," and it was widely distributed and read.

## Enormous Changes

The 1621 "Pilgrim and Indian" Thanksgiving story emerged in the late 1800s, a time of enormous changes in America—mass immigration that brought over 25 million, mostly non–English-speaking people; rapid industrialization that created great gaps in wealth; explosive urbanization that created cities teeming with people; and an imperialistic foreign policy that gave America control over Puerto Rico, Guam, and the Philippines.

These changes caused many anxieties and tensions. For example, at a time when most Americans were English-speaking Protestants from northern Europe, the mass immigration brought millions of mostly non–English-speaking people of diverse faiths from southern and eastern Europe. The rapid industrialization created great disparity of income and increased class conflict. The explosive urbanization left many families barely surviving in harsh living conditions. The imperialistic foreign policy had people in other countries (and some Americans, including Mark Twain and Helen Keller) worried that America was bent on global domination.

Americans were ready for a story, one that would help relieve their anxieties and tensions. The "Pilgrim and Indian" Thanksgiving story had a lot to offer. It is a triumphant and celebratory story about surviving hard times. It is a story of the Pilgrims—English-speaking people from northern Europe, who were Protestant—inviting the Indians to their feast (a reassuring image to counter America's imperialistic foreign policy and perhaps gloss over the subsequent fate of Native Americans). It is a story about food and family in an austere setting and is about giving thanks.

## Spreading the Story

American schools were—and still are—the primary vehicle for disseminating the "Pilgrim and Indian" Thanksgiving story. Beginning in 1900, articles about how to teach the story appeared in publications for elementary schoolteachers. In 1906, A. W. Greeley wrote in the *Washington Post,* "the feast with Massasoit and his Indian guests . . . is now a familiar schoolroom classic."

In 1910, Margaret Pumphrey wrote *Stories of the Pilgrims.* A popular book, illustrated by Lucy Fitch Perkins, it was one of the sources of several myths, including the depiction of the Indians wearing full war bonnets to the Thanksgiving feast. The book also claimed that the Indians introduced the Pilgrims to popcorn and reported that Massasoit "ate the puffy dumplings in Priscilla's stew" and said "Ugh! The Great Spirit loves his white children best!"

By the 1920s, the "Pilgrim and Indian" story was a standard feature in history textbooks. In one textbook, students learned that "Governor Bradford set aside a day of Thanksgiving as the President does to-day. Together with Indian guests, the Pilgrims feasted for a week on corn, squash, and pumpkin, on wild fowl, and on deer." According to another textbook, "When the winter's supply of wood and food had been stored away, Governor Bradford appointed a day of Thanksgiving. All their Indian friends were invited to the feast. Everyone contributed and had a share in the good times. This was the first Thanksgiving ever celebrated in America."

## Yearly Pageants

Year after year, the "Pilgrim and Indian" Thanksgiving story was reenacted in school pageants throughout America. Getting children to dress up like Pilgrims and Indians and reenact the event in classroom and community programs was a powerful way to spread the story into the popular culture. A newspaper article published on November 17, 1940, advised its readers that "practically every well-run school program features that perennial favorite . . . the First Thanksgiving. . . . There are little boys in high cardboard hats and silver cardboard buckles. Little girls trip on long gray skirts. And the Indians in crepe paper say, majestically, 'Me Massasoit, me great chief,' or, less impressively, 'Me Squanto, me friendly.'"

Typically, there were more Pilgrims than Indians in the pageants, although in fact there were many more Indians at the feast in 1621. The male Pilgrim actors always wore black clothes and a high hat with a silver buckle. The majority of teens and adults who took my survey agreed that was what Pilgrim men wore. The majority also thought Pilgrim women wore black clothes and a white apron. However, the evidence from historical records reveals that black was not the typical color of the Pilgrims' clothes, nor were there any high hats with a silver buckle. Women commonly wore clothes that ranged from red to brown to violet. Men typically wore white, beige, and earthy green. On their heads, men wore a felt hat or cap. Women wore a bonnet or a hat. Girls wore dresses, and so did boys until they were about eight years old. Children's clothes came in many colors—blue, yellow, red, and brown.

Although parts of this photograph are blurry, I selected it because it shows an early—1904—Thanksgiving Day Pageant at Maxfield School in St. Paul, Minnesota. It's interesting to note that there are no children dressed as Indians. Also note the children sitting with their hands folded. The bottle on the corner of each desk contains ink.

## Americanization

During the first two decades of the 1900s, an Americanization movement thrived in the United States. Classes were held in many places, including factories, schools, churches and synagogues, and immigration stations such as Ellis Island. Immigrants were pressured to attend Americanization classes where they

During World War II, the United States government forced more than 100,000 Japanese Americans, two thirds of whom were American citizens, into internment camps. This picture was taken at the Gila River Relocation Center, Rivers, Arizona, on Thanksgiving Day, 1942, when the "evacuees" (the government's term) held a daylong celebration that included a church service, parade, and dance. There were many floats in the parade, including this turkey float with evacuee children dressed as Pilgrims and Indians.

were taught English and instructed in American ideals and traditions and history, including, of course, the 1621 Thanksgiving story. Interestingly, some immigrants, including my own mother, who came from what is now the Czech Republic, embraced the "Pilgrim and Indian" story. Immigrants could identify with the

Pilgrims, who, after all, were immigrants too. They related to their hardship and suffering. In order to survive, many immigrants knew that they would have to learn things from the Americans, just as the Pilgrims had to learn things from the Indians. The image of friendly Indians was undoubtedly reassuring to immigrants, who hoped that Americans would likewise be friendly to them. During its heyday, the Americanization movement spread the 1621 "Pilgrim and Indian" story to millions of immigrants and their children.

For many Native Americans, however, the association of the Thanksgiving celebration with the 1621 event was troubling in light of their treatment throughout American history. In 1970, the 350th anniversary of the landing of the *Mayflower* was celebrated. Frank James, a leader of the Wampanoag known as Wamsutta, made a bold statement. He had been invited by officials of the Commonwealth of Massachusetts to speak at the annual Thanksgiving dinner at Plymouth. Before the event, an official asked James for a copy of his speech. After reading the speech, the official told him that he could not deliver it because it was "inflammatory." In part of his speech, James had written:

> It is with mixed emotion that I stand here to share
> my thoughts. This is a time of celebration for
> you—celebrating an anniversary of a beginning
> for the white man in America. A time of looking
> back, of reflection. It is with a heavy heart that I
> look back upon what happened to my People. . . .
> History gives us facts and there were atrocities;

there were broken promises. . . . Our spirit refuses
to die. Yesterday we walked the woodland paths
and sandy trails. Today we must walk the
macadam highways and roads. We are uniting. . . .
We stand tall and proud, and before too many
moons pass we'll right the wrongs we have
allowed to happen to us.

The official offered to revise the speech. James refused. Instead
of going to the dinner, he went to the statue of Massasoit that
stands on Cole's Hill in Plymouth and gave his speech to a group
of supporters, thus beginning a tradition that continues today.
Every year at noon on Thanksgiving, a group of Native Americans and their supporters gather on Cole's Hill in Plymouth to
commemorate a National Day of Mourning. The flyer for the
event in 2006 read, in part, "Participants in National Day of
Mourning honor Native ancestors and the struggles of Native
peoples to survive today."

First-grade students at school #42 in Indianapolis, Indiana, dressed as Pilgrims and an Indian for a Thanksgiving Day program in 1965. The boat is the *Mayflower*. The wall behind them is decorated with Thanksgiving artwork, including two cornucopias. The poster on the easel in the right side of the picture reads "The Indians. The Indians were / kind to the Pilgrims. / They taught them / how to plant their crops. / The Indians danced / for the pilgrim children. / The Indians taught / the Pilgrim children / games."

**NATIONAL DAY OF MOURNING**

Since 1970, Native Americans have gathered at noon on Cole's Hill in Plymouth to commemorate a National Day of Mourning on the U.S. Thanksgiving holiday. Many Native Americans do not celebrate the arrival of the Pilgrims and other European settlers. To them, Thanksgiving Day is a reminder of the genocide of millions of their people, the theft of their lands, and the relentless assault on their culture. Participants in National Day of Mourning honor Native ancestors and the struggles of Native peoples to survive today. It is a day of remembrance and spiritual connection as well as a protest of the racism and oppression which Native Americans continue to experience.

Erected by the Town of Plymouth on behalf of the United American Indians of New England

A plaque commemorating the National Day of Mourning is attached to a boulder near the statue of Massasoit on Cole's Hill, in Plymouth, Massachusetts. The insert is the front of the plaque.

PART II

# THANKSGIVING TRADITIONS

FIVE

# GATHERINGS:
# Family and Friends

Many people who returned my survey wrote about spending Thanksgiving with family and friends. "Thanksgiving is a time for everyone in the family to come together and enjoy a good time and to be around people who love and care about you," wrote sixteen-year-old Caleb Raymond. "I absolutely love this holiday . . . the relaxed attitude of the day—the gathering of children and grandchildren," wrote seventy-year-old Jennie Lou Fredle Klim. Angie Schumucker wrote, "Thanksgiving was always a time that Mom invited everyone (or so it seemed) to our home so that no one would be without a place to celebrate. We had everyone from my eighty-something-year-old piano teacher, single adults from church, married couples with no children, to the in-laws of my aunts. There were often thirty or forty people, and we generally had tables everywhere, including the garage."

## For Me Too

Thanksgiving has always meant family and friends for me too. During my growing-up years, it also meant an unusual mix of people at our Thanksgiving table. That is because, for many years,

*Thanksgiving Day—Arrival at the Old Home*, by Winslow Homer, appeared in *Harper's Weekly*, November 27, 1858.

my family lived on the grounds of a state mental hospital, where my father was a psychiatrist. Some patients worked in our house (a practice that was considered beneficial at that time but was later stopped because it was seen as exploitative, since the patients were not paid). At Thanksgiving, the patients who worked at our house joined us for Thanksgiving dinner. So did doctors who had come from other countries—Turkey and India— to study psychiatry with my father.

## Over the River

The tradition of people gathering on Thanksgiving is captured in the classic poem by Lydia Maria Child that begins "Over the river, and through the wood." Born in Massachusetts in 1802, Child was a versatile author who fought against slavery and for women's rights and started the first children's magazine in America. As a young person, I learned part of Child's poem as a song and later passed it on to my children. However, I did not know until I wrote this book that it was originally titled "The New-England Boy's Song: About Thanksgiving Day" and that there are twelve verses, ten more than I learned! I also did not know that it was about going to "grandfather's house" because we always sang "to grandmother's house." Most people, including me and my children, only sang the first and the third verses. A 1927 schoolbook my mother used included the poem with the title "Thanksgiving Day" and verses one, three, five, eight, nine, and twelve of the original poem. Here are all twelve verses as Child published them in 1845, numbered so you can see what most people, and perhaps you, sang, and what was reprinted in my mother's schoolbook.

28    THE NEW-ENGLAND BOY'S SONG.

Over the river, and through the wood—
When grandmother sees us come,
She will say, Oh dear,
The children are here,
Bring a pie for every one.

Over the river, and through the wood—
Now grandmother's cap I spy!
Hurra for the fun!
Is the pudding done?
Hurra for the pumpkin pie!

The original text and illustration for the last two stanzas of "The New-England Boy's Song" in Lydia Maria Child's book *Flowers for Children*.

1. Over the river, and through the wood,
   To grandfather's house we go;
   The horse knows the way,
   To carry the sleigh,
   Through the white and drifted snow.

2. Over the river, and through the wood,
   to grandfather's house away!
   We would not stop
   For doll or top,
   For 't is Thanksgiving Day.

3. Over the river, and through the wood,
   Oh, how the wind does blow!
   It stings the toes,
   And bites the nose,
   As over the ground we go.

4. Over the river, and through the wood,
   With a clear blue winter sky,
   The dogs do bark,
   And the children hark,
   As we go jingling by.

5. Over the river, and through the wood,
   To have a first-rate play—
   Hear the bells ring,
   Ting a ling ding,
   Hurra for Thanksgiving Day!

6. Over the river, and through the wood—
   No matter for winds that blow;
   Or if we get
   The sleigh upset,
   Into a bank of snow.

7. Over the river, and through the wood,
   To see little John and Ann;
   We will kiss them all,
   And play snow ball,
   And stay as long as we can.

8. Over the river, and through the wood,
   Trot fast, my dapple-gray!
   Spring over the ground,
   Like a hunting hound,
   For 't is Thanksgiving Day!

9. Over the river, and through the wood,
   And straight through the barnyard gate;
   We seem to go
   Extremely slow,
   It is so hard to wait.

10. Over the river, and through the wood—
    Old Jowler hears our bells;
    He shakes his paw,
    With a loud bow wow,
    And thus the news he tells.

11. Over the river, and through the wood—
    When grandmother sees us come,
    She will say, Oh dear,
    The children are here,
    Bring a pie for every one.

12. Over the river, and through the wood—
    Now grandmother's cap I spy!
    Hurra for the fun!
    Is the pudding done?
    Hurra for the pumpkin pie!

## Steamboats, Stagecoaches, Railroads

By the mid-1800s, improvements in transportation made it easier for families to be reunited on Thanksgiving. In the West, the number of steamboats carrying passengers on rivers and canals jumped from 17 to 727 between 1817 and 1855. More roads were being built for wagons and stagecoaches pulled by teams of horses or oxen. By the late 1830s, the National Road, or Cumberland Road, as it was also called, extended from Maryland to Vandalia, Illinois. Of course, roads were also used by many people traveling on horseback. The first trains in America had started to operate in 1830; by 1850, there was an extensive railroad system that connected towns and cities. Within two decades, a transcontinental railroad was completed. All this made it possible for many Americans to "come home" for Thanksgiving.

Another poem, "Thanksgiving Song," reflected the social and

*Home to Thanksgiving,* a popular and widely reproduced lithograph published by Currier & Ives in the mid-1860s.

economic changes taking place in America. It appeared in the November 20, 1856, issue of *The Youth's Companion,* a widely read and influential magazine. At this time, traditional ways of earning a living on the family farm were disappearing and new ways were being created in businesses and factories. While the older generation might have stayed on the farm, many in the younger generation—both men and women—had to seek work elsewhere. With families scattered, many people must have felt a longing for one another, a longing that undoubtedly prompted them to embrace the idea of a holiday that brought everyone home. (Remember that at the same time this poem was published, Sarah Josepha Hale was writing that one of the benefits of Thanksgiving was to reunite families.) Here are two verses of "Thanksgiving Song":

> Come, uncles and cousins; come, nieces and aunts;
> Come, nephews and brothers,—no *wonts* and
>     no *cants*;
> Put business, and shopping, and school-books away;
> The year has rolled round;—it is Thanksgiving-day.
>
> Come home from the college, ye ringlet-haired
>     youth,
> Come home from your factories, Ann, Kate,
>     and Ruth;
> From the anvil, the counter, the farm come away;
> Home, home with you, home;—it is
>     Thanksgiving-day.

According to C. H. Rockwell, a commander in the United States Navy, during his boyhood in the mid-1850s, "it was always

When You go Home for Thanksgiving

Don't fail to take some of our beautiful Flowers.

Chrysanthemums, 3 for 50 Cts., 12 for $2.00. Largest Flowers 25 Cents each. Chrysanthemums, Pompones 50 Cts. pr. bunch.

Carnations, assorted colors. $1 per Dozen.

Roses, $1. $1.50 and $2 per Doz. Assorted boxes and baskets of exceptional value $1 each.

Poinsetta Plants, 25 and 50 Cts. each.

Crysanthemum Plants, 75 Cts. each.

Don't Fail to take or send some of our Flowers Home for Thanksgiving.

THE FLOWER SHOP | Bancrofts Green House,
216 Main. | 12th & Tremont St.

A picture of a rose was used to entice college students heading home for Thanksgiving in this advertisement from a flower shop in a 1916 issue of the *College Eye,* the student newspaper at the University of Northern Iowa. The most popular flower for Thanksgiving decorations was the chrysanthemum, a flower that blooms in the fall.

Thanksgiving Dinner at the "children's table," a familiar tradition in many families. This picture was taken on Thanksgiving in 1940 at the home of the Crouch family in Ledyard, Connecticut.

considered obligatory to gather at the homestead on Thanksgiving day if possible. From the far West, from the South, from New England, sons and daughters with all their children met under the old roof."

## Away from Home

But what about people who could not come home?

Many people eagerly celebrated Thanksgiving wherever they were. Sarah Josepha Hale published reports of Americans celebrating abroad, as did various newspapers. One year, a newspaper reported that five hundred Americans celebrated Thanksgiving at a hotel in London, England. Three hundred Americans celebrated in Berlin, Germany. In Rome, Italy, "Hundreds of Stars and Stripes hanging from the houses of Americans announced Thanksgiving Day to the people here." Another year there were reports of Americans celebrating in Havana, Cuba.

In the late 1890s, May Albertina "Minnie" Hawthorne, her husband, Julian (the son of the famous writer Nathaniel Hawthorne and his wife, Sophia Peabody), and their many children were living in Jamaica. "One day," Minnie Hawthorne later wrote, "while the tropic sun was shining, the palm-trees waving, the banana leaves expanding and the humming-birds whirring and poising about the chocho blossoms, some one said, 'Day after to-morrow is Thanksgiving!' . . . Day after to-morrow! There was no time to be lost. Urgent inquiry revealed the existence of a turkey at a place nine miles distant. The horses were put to the buggy. . . . The place was found, the turkey . . . at the cost of an hour's diplomatic wheedling and three dollars, was secured."

During World War II, the United States government distributed photographs to encourage people to support the war effort. This picture of a family gathering to eat their turkey dinner in a defense factory was taken on Thanksgiving Day, 1942. The caption under the picture reads "American workers give up the holiday to speed victory. The Blackwelder family celebrated Thanksgiving at their benches in a Glenn Martin Company plant. William P. Blackwelder works in the tool crib of the plane factory, and his wife and daughter are riveters. A son, Frank, in the Navy for one year, has been wounded."

As for making pumpkin pies, Minnie Hawthorne reported that there were plenty of pumpkins "growing on a vine which crept along the terrace behind the kitchen." She sent the younger children to the henhouse to collect eggs. The neighbors' cow provided the milk. A "tiny sieve two inches in diameter" was used to sift the flour, and "a bottle filled with cold spring water" was turned into a rolling pin. The pies were put in an old oven with a wood door, where they "baked admirably." For table decoration, the family "went forth upon the hillsides and hedges, and gathered wild smilax, maidenhair and tree-ferns, flowering orchids by the handful, gorgeous masses of purple, scarlet and yellow pepper branches, wild scarlet salvia and palms."

Their menu included "fresh green peas, new potatoes and cucumbers." The only problem was the weather: "It was difficult," Hawthorne wrote, "to imagine the snow-covered fields, the leafless woods and the chill winds of our native Thanksgiving." But then, she concluded, for ten minutes a brief rain squall swept by and their desire for difficult weather on Thanksgiving was satisfied.

Of course, many people who spend Thanksgiving away from home may feel sad or lonely. The Reverend R. F. Putnam, a New Englander who lived in California, wrote this entry in his diary in 1863: "Thanksgiving, which was here as in Massachusetts, on the 16th of November, was a solemn and unsatisfactory day. . . . We thought of home and longed to be there. . . . Our dinner was plain and simple, for we had no heart for a sumptuous repast. We had been invited to dine out, but declined all such invitations, preferring to remain alone and think of the dear ones who gathered around the Thanksgiving table at home."

Although it may seem as if I am ending this chapter on a down note, I know from my own experience that celebrating Thanksgiving can be complicated, even painful, for so many reasons. In my family, like most families, we've had to deal with everything from the deaths of one of my brothers when he was twenty years old and my father when he was fifty, to divorce, to children growing up and spending Thanksgiving elsewhere. But I also know from my own experience that families go on—new partnerships and marriages are formed, babies are born—and new friends are found. And so we continue the tradition of coming together for Thanksgiving.

# SIX

# ACTIVITIES:
# Good Deeds, Football, and Parades

*Solemn*—that word frequently appeared in early Thanksgiving Proclamations. It appeared in the proclamation issued by the governing council of Charlestown, Massachusetts, on June 20, 1676. It appeared in capital letters—SOLEMN THANKSGIVING—in the first national Thanksgiving Proclamation issued by the Continental Congress. President George Washington used it, as did his successor, John Adams.

## Holy Day to Holiday

By the late 1600s, however, people were spending less time practicing the solemn traditions of attending church and praying on days of thanksgiving. Young people, in particular, were more inclined to socialize with one another and play games. In an effort to enforce solemn observances, laws were passed in Massachusetts, New Hampshire, and Connecticut that, for example, instructed people not to "Use any Game, Sport, Play, or Recreation on . . . Thanksgiving . . . on pain that every Person so Offending shall for every offence Forfeit the Sum of Ten Shillings." But those laws were last-gasp efforts to stop the shift from a religious to an increasingly secular Thanksgiving Day. "The holy day was becoming a holiday" is how Diana Karter Appelbaum described the shift.

This shift reflected larger changes. By the 1660s, religion had become less important in people's lives. Religious differences, of course, existed among the Separatists (later known as Pilgrims) and the majority of other passengers on the *Mayflower*. Although the Separatists' quest for religious freedom is a central story in American history, the fact is that many of the passengers were not seeking religious freedom. Some of them, whom the Separatists called Strangers, were seeking economic opportunities. The Separatists had hired others to provide various services, including Miles Standish, a professional soldier who served as their military leader, and John Alden, a skilled craftsman.

Another crucial change was increasing prosperity in the New England colonies. Many people were making money by buying and selling goods. Trade—in, for example, grain, horses, fish, rum, molasses, and slaves—was flourishing between the colonies and England and the West Indies. Mansions were being built in Boston, Massachusetts, Newport, Rhode Island, and Charleston, South Carolina.

These changes, of course, did not mean that Americans stopped going to church on Thanksgiving Day. They did go, but by the early 1700s Thanksgiving dinner had become a more elaborate and lengthy affair, while church services were shorter.

Along with a Thanksgiving feast, often came fun. Families played parlor games—charades, chess, checkers, cards—told stories, sang around the piano, and danced. They looked at family

*Thanksgiving-Day—Blindman's-Bluff* appeared in *Harper's Weekly* in 1857.

albums and scrapbooks. Children played in the snow and went sledding and took sleigh rides. Visiting friends was also a popular activity. "Ah, it is a glad *Thanksgiving day*," wrote one poet, Mrs. R. N. Turner. "And dear old friends are meeting. . . . Such gleeful merry-making!/ Such shouts, such mirth, from morn to night."

By the mid-1800s, people started attending concerts, plays, and the opera on Thanksgiving Day. The dancing people did in their parlors soon evolved into organized events that ranged from fancy balls to informal folk dancing. Fancy balls remained popular into the early 1900s. The hostess of one ball provided vegetable costumes for the guests. Women could be a radish—"bright red skirt surmounted by a deep neck ruff or bodice formed of green

*Thanksgiving Day—The Dance* depicts an exuberant group of young and old people. It was published in *Harper's Weekly*, November 27, 1858.

leaves . . . red cotton filled paper radishes are to be worn as earrings." The "fluffy head of lettuce" costume consisted of a "skirt and bodice made of overlapped layers of crinkly green paper." Men could choose a cucumber, ear of corn, carrot, or stalk of celery costume, all of which were made from long pieces of paper with stripes, including "dark green paper slightly striped and dotted" for the cucumber. The carrot costume was made from "vivid yellow paper with faintly outlined stripes" and had a "pointed headdress, topped with green."

## Good Deeds

This type of Thanksgiving—feasting and fun—was, of course, beyond the reach of most poor people, and folks with plenty were urged to be charitable on Thanksgiving. "Many people spend this day in a very wicked manner," the editors of *The Youth's Companion* admonished readers. "They seek only to please themselves and never think of thanking God, or making their fellow beings happy. I hope none of you will be so wicked. . . . Have you not some poor neighbor who needs a part of your abundance?"

A poem titled "Thanksgiving" included these lines:

> This week is *Thanksgiving*, and oh, what a time!
> . . .
> Plum-puddings and tarts and nice jellies abound,
> To grace the rich harvest secured from the ground;
> . . .
> Dear children, remember how many there are
> Who have no home to go to, no table to share,
> No parents to gather them into their fold,
> To shield them from danger, or keep them from cold.
>
> O think of those comfortless children, I say,
> And save them your pennies—not waste them in play,
> And if you have not e'en a penny to spare,
> You can give them a blessing! Oh, give them
>    a prayer!

Charitable giving remained a big part of Thanksgiving throughout the 1800s. In 1879, George Augustus Sala, an English journalist, spent Thanksgiving Day in New York City. He reported that

> the destitute and the infirm, the prisoners and
> captives were abundantly fed . . . a volunteer

choir . . . perambulated the gloomy corridors of
the prison, singing glees for the solace of the
prisoners. The children in the reformatories and
industrial schools, and the poor little urchins in
the asylum of the Five Points Mission, all held
high festival. . . . They tell me that there is a great

This engraving, *Thanksgiving Sketches*, appeared in *Harper's Weekly*, December 8, 1866. The captions for
the side panels illustrate four aspects of Thanksgiving: top left caption reads "The Preparation";
bottom left reads "Arrival Home"; top right reads "Frolic with the Children"; bottom right reads "After
Dinner." The middle panels depict the difference between "The Rich Man's Turkey" (top) and "The
Poor Man's Turkey" (bottom). During the 1800s, some magazines regularly published illustrations,
poems, and stories that reminded rich people to be charitable on Thanksgiving Day.

In the mid-1800s, members of the Ladies' Home Missionary Society of the Methodist Episcopal Church started a school that provided education, religion, food, clothing, and soap and water for poor children in the area of lower Manhattan known as Five Points. On Thanksgiving, the ladies and men who supported their work served dinner to thousands of children (note that the children are standing to eat). Merchants, hotels, and private families donated food and money. Crowds of people would come to observe the event. This engraving, *Thanksgiving Dinner at the Five Points Ladies' Home Mission of the Methodist Episcopal Church*, appeared in *Harper's Weekly*, December 23, 1865.

deal of misery in New York: but, to all appearance, the Good Samaritan is out and about in every street of the Great City on Thursday.

Being charitable continues to be an important Thanksgiving Day tradition. Today people volunteer to serve Thanksgiving dinners in homeless shelters and soup kitchens. They make special visits to nursing homes and hospitals. People donate money. Many people, like Julie Hemming Savage's family in Silver Spring, Maryland, welcome a variety of guests for Thanksgiving—"The house is always full because we invite a bunch of other people who don't have a place to go for Thanksgiving." Anne Chang, who teaches at Ramapo College of New Jersey in Mahwah, New Jersey, also has "a varying guest list—usually people who are international students or others who don't go to family for this holiday."

## Sports

By the mid-1800s, baseball was a popular Thanksgiving Day activity for players and spectators. Rounders, an English game also known as town ball, had been played since the 1700s. Players used a bat and ball and ran around bases. To make an "out," a fielder had to hit the base runner with the ball, known as "soaking" or "plugging" the runner. Tagging runners replaced "soaking" sometime in the early 1840s.

About the time baseball became popular, men began playing a game they called football. During the Civil War, a Union soldier wrote in his diary, "We had an excellent dinner here Thanksgiving Day, Turkey, Chicken pies, cakes, nuts, apples, and everything nice. We have the best kind of time. We have foot Ball and we have a good deal of fun with it. The boys are taking a game now."

The first college football game—Rutgers defeated the College of New Jersey (now called Princeton University)—was played on November 6, 1869, four years after the Civil War ended. Within a decade, the championship game between the two best Ivy League

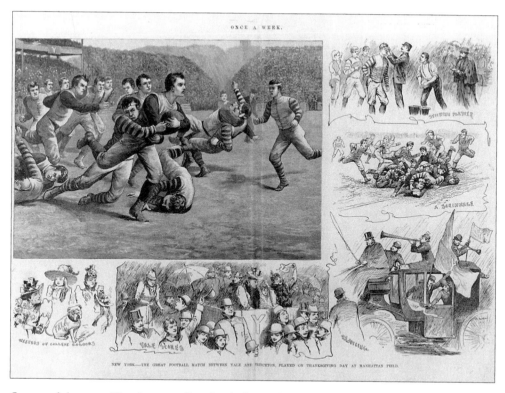

Scenes of the great Thanksgiving Day football match between Yale and Princeton, 1891.

college teams was held on Thanksgiving Day in New York City. Usually Princeton and Yale played. As many as 40,000 spectators packed the stadium. Elsewhere in the country, other football teams scheduled their "big" game for Thanksgiving Day too. "Thanksgiving Day is no longer a solemn festival to God for mercies given," wrote one newspaper editor. "It is a holiday granted by the State and the Nation to see a game of football."

Before long, high school football teams were playing on Thanksgiving, usually against a big rival or for a championship. Dot Emer has never forgotten a high school Thanksgiving Day game she attended in 1949. "We lost at the last minute, thirteen–fourteen! We were all heartbroken, and I still remember that awful feeling of losing our last football game, especially since we always had a championship team. And that was almost fifty-seven years ago!"

In my family, we did not go to football games on Thanksgiving—we played the annual "Toilet Bowl" with a group of friends. My brother Vin started the tradition in the early 1960s. He dubbed it the "Toilet Bowl" the year he found a toilet seat on the field where we played. There were no benches or bleachers, just a toilet seat that everyone took turns sitting on.

George Richards scheduled the first professional football game played on Thanksgiving. The year was 1934 and Richards was the new owner of the Spartans, a football team in Ohio that he renamed the Lions and moved to Detroit, Michigan. Richards arranged to have the game broadcast on the radio station that he also owned. Through a network of radio stations, the game was broadcast across America. With the growing popularity of television in the 1950s, watching football on television became synonymous with Thanksgiving, a tradition that evoked different responses from people who answered my survey. "Great day for football!" wrote M. Jerry Weiss. Meg Ferron and her family always "watch the Detroit Lions play football." Lisa Rexford finds this tradition "so annoying—I'm trying to have a nice dinner and the game is on!" Doris Weatherford thinks "Football has taken too great a role. They can have the rest of the weekend—no games on Thanksgiving Day!"

## Fantastics

In the late 1700s, a Thanksgiving tradition developed that lasted more than a hundred years before disappearing. Fantastics or Fantasticals—groups of men wearing outlandish costumes—paraded through the streets of New York City and parts of Pennsylvania on Thanksgiving morning. Many Fantasticals dressed as women. They were rowdy and noisy—shouting, yelling, and blowing horns. One newspaper described a Fantastical parade as "a mass of moving, shouting beings, whose costumes were as varied as the whims of a coquette, dazzling the eye with the variegated brilliancy of a kaleidoscope, flitted about on the dancing platform." Fantasticals were usually men who worked at jobs such as selling fish, guarding prisons, or hawking goods from a cart.

A lithograph of a Fantastical parade in New York City, December 2, 1833.

The Fantasticals belonged to companies with names such as Ham Guard Warriors, Gilhooley Musketeers, and the Secondhand Lumberdealers Association. By the 1880s, more than fifty Fantastical companies marched in New York City on Thanksgiving Day. "When the procession started," wrote a newspaper reporter, "the people on the sidewalks set up a yell and the bands of musicians worked with a will. . . . [Then] came . . . robbers, pirates, fiends, devils, imps, fairies, priests, bishops, gypsies, flower girls, kings, clowns, princes, jesters." After the parade, which lasted until midafternoon, the Fantasticals congregated in public parks to drink and eat and celebrate. At night, they danced at balls all over the city.

Where did the idea of Fantasticals originate? Some historians connect them to the English tradition of "masquerading door to door for treats" on Guy Fawkes Day, the old English holiday that marks the foiling of a plot to blow up the Houses of Parliament.

## Ragamuffins

Children dressed up too, in clothes they borrowed from their parents or older siblings. "I would wear my brother's old suits and pants," recalled Celeste Schamel, who grew up in Brooklyn in the early 1900s. "You put dirt all over your face . . . your hair was all up under the cap. . . . We would go out of our neighborhood . . . all working people. . . . So we would go to the other side of Prospect Park [to an affluent area]. . . . We would go *there* and bang on the door. Now, you never took money. You took fruit or food, some kind of cookies or fruit. And the thing you would say,

A group of ragamuffins.

'Got anything for Thanksgiving?'" Dubbed "ragamuffins," groups of these children appeared on the sidewalks of all the boroughs of New York City, as well as Jersey City and Hoboken, New Jersey.

By the early 1900s, public opinion shifted. The Fantasticals were viewed as out of control and a threat to an orderly society. Pressure was put on the police to crack down on their behavior. Attitudes about ragamuffins shifted too. The tradition was now viewed as teaching children to beg. A group of leading citizens wrote in a letter to a newspaper, "Surely . . . to teach young children to become beggars is no right use of our National day of prayer and thanksgiving." In time, the traditions of Fantasticals and ragamuffins ended.

## Parades

Fantasticals and ragamuffins may have disappeared, but the idea of parades reappeared in 1920 when Gimbel's department store in Philadelphia sponsored a parade as a way to promote the holiday shopping season. Four years later, the J. L. Hudson department

In the 1900s, the consumer culture (a culture in which merchants and advertisers attempt to persuade people to buy more things than they need) in America was accelerated by new advertising tactics that included commercializing holidays. For Thanksgiving that meant creating cards and table decorations and parades that featured Santa Claus as a way to jump-start the holiday buying season. This Santa Claus arrived in St. Paul, Minnesota, on Thanksgiving Day in 1936.

store held a Thanksgiving parade in Detroit. That same day, Macy's in New York City sponsored what they called the "Macy's Christmas Day Parade," in anticipation of the big shopping holiday. (It was renamed the Macy's Thanksgiving Day Parade in 1927.) Soon department stores across America were sponsoring parades on Thanksgiving Day. Over the years, however, parades became too expensive for most department stores to sponsor. Today the Macy's parade is the premier parade that is watched by millions of spectators in person or on television. "When my three sisters and I were younger, going to the Macy's Parade was a tradition," Suzanne Hellman wrote on her survey. "My cousins were always part of it (clowns or extras on floats). . . . Now we watch it on TV." Heather Nevis-Sosnovsky wrote, "My favorite Thanksgiving tradition is the parade."

## Variety of Activities

On their survey, many people described a variety of Thanksgiving Day activities. Some young people wrote about school activities such as "making little Pilgrim hats out of paper." Amanda Tiffany wrote of learning "how to make paper turkeys by tracing our hands." The adults wrote about visiting family graves, taking long walks, catching up with family and friends, and playing games. Julie Hemming Savage wrote that she and her family "visit the National Zoo [in Washington, D.C.] Thanksgiving morning while the turkey is in the oven." Regardless of what people have done and continue to do on Thanksgiving Day, I was struck by the fact that all the activities in one way or another involve other people—a fitting theme, it seems to me, for Thanksgiving Day.

# SEVEN

# FOOD:
# Turkey and Lasagna

Once, only once, in my lifetime did I *not* eat turkey on Thanksgiving. That was the year one of my brothers-in-law insisted on cooking steaks. The only turkeys on the table were miniature chocolate ones! On the way home, my family and I agreed that a Thanksgiving dinner without turkey was *not* a Thanksgiving dinner.

## Wild Turkey

Many people think turkey was on the menu at the 1621 event. But was it? It could have been: There were plenty of wild turkeys in the woods around Plymouth. The Wampanoag hunted and ate them. In his firsthand report of the event, Edward Winslow wrote that the colonists killed many "fowl." Unfortunately, he did not specify what kind, and there were many types of fowl in the waters and woods around Plymouth—ducks, geese, ruffed grouse, bobwhites, also heath hens and passenger pigeons, both of which are now extinct. Today, the question is still being debated.

[RIGHT] In the early 1900s, the first Thanksgiving Day cards began to be sold. This turkey family appeared on a card in 1907.

[BELOW] By 1910, merchants were trying to extend the Christmas holiday buying season to begin at Halloween. This 1911 Thanksgiving Day card includes the symbols of Halloween (black cat and pumpkin), a turkey for Thanksgiving, and *joyous*— a word associated with Christmas.

### Turkeys and Thanksgiving

Turkeys were first domesticated, or farm-raised, in Mexico. In the early 1500s, Spanish explorers brought these turkeys to Europe. From there, these turkeys spread to other parts of the world. Turkeys were part of Americans' Thanksgiving feast by the early 1700s, and they were served along with other meat and fowl and seafood, including roast pork, roast beef, duck, and lobster.

By the late 1800s, however, a roasted turkey had become the centerpiece of the dinner. In part, according to business historian Thomas DiBacco, this was because a group of poultry producers launched a marketing campaign during the post–Civil War years to get Americans to eat more turkey, especially at Thanksgiving. Their efforts coincided with the appearance of turkeys—live and roasted—in depictions of Thanksgiving Day in paintings, magazines, newspapers, and books.

On my survey I asked people what they ate for Thanksgiving; 100 percent of the teens and 95 percent of the adults answered turkey. Some people indicated that although they serve other meats—ham, roast beef, lamb, chicken—a roasted turkey is still the featured meat.

During a long period when she was a vegetarian, Sandip Wilson and her vegetarian friends ate "a mound of tofu that looked like a turkey, complete with stuffing. The 'turkey' was beautifully seasoned with rosemary, thyme, sage, and displayed in the middle of the table on a huge oval plate decorated with vegetables, greenery, and cherry tomatoes for color."

## Regional Differences

Along with a turkey, most people who responded to my survey indicated that the following foods are served at their Thanksgiving dinner: stuffing, gravy, white potatoes, sweet potatoes, cranberry sauce, pumpkin pie, and apple pie. Other foods included broccoli, peas, green beans, pearl onions in cream sauce, squash, and turnips. Doris Weatherford wrote about the regional differences she experienced growing up: "After we moved from Minnesota to Arkansas when I was ten, other people considered cornbread stuffing to be a must [her mother used white

These turkeys are eating their Thanksgiving dinner, instead of being eaten. That's the philosophy of Adopt-A-Turkey, a Farm Sanctuary program that offers people an opportunity to adopt a turkey. Farm Sanctuary was established in 1986 to advocate for the humane treatment of farm animals.

bread]. . . . Pecan pie also was a Southern must-have, as well as candied sweet potatoes." David Skurnick connected the ham on his family's Thanksgiving menu to his mother's Southern roots. Sweet potato pie and macaroni and cheese were on Crystal Lewis-Colman's list, a legacy of her mother's ancestors who lived in South Carolina.

My experience with regional difference occurred when I lived in Oklahoma City, Oklahoma, and discovered that okra— raw, marinated, or breaded and fried—was a staple on the Thanksgiving dinner menu. As I was writing this book, I read a newspaper article, "Why Have Turkey If There's Whale?," about the foods that are eaten for Thanksgiving in the native villages in Alaska, including Nuiqsut. In addition to the traditional turkey and mashed potatoes, there are "delicacies such as reindeer stew, moose roast, stuffed moose heart, and whale blubber salad. For dessert, there might be akutaq, which is whipped animal or vegetable fat that is mixed with sugar, berries, and sometimes fish."

A conversation with a group of elementary schoolteachers alerted me to some of the ways in which ethnic foods have expanded the traditional Thanksgiving menu, a practice that, for much of our history, was discouraged. For example, during the early 1900s, a time of mass immigration, newly arriving immigrants were given courses in how to cook traditional Thanksgiving Day foods. In 1920 a newspaper reported: "Over on Ellis Island about 1,000 immigrants will get an Americanization course of turkey. . . . Their studies will be entitled Roast Jersey Turkey, Mashed Potatoes, Cranberry Sauce, Bread and Its Relations to Butter, Mince Pie and Coffee."

## Ethnic Foods

Although many immigrants and their descendants embraced the traditional Thanksgiving foods, many of them included—and still do—their own ethnic foods too. Voula Parliaros, an elementary schoolteacher, said that her mother spends several days before Thanksgiving making traditional Greek dishes—*pastitsio* and *spanakopita*—along with the traditional Thanksgiving foods. Another teacher described how her family celebrates their Italian heritage by making a Thanksgiving feast of Italian dishes—antipasti and lasagna—"with a turkey on the side that no one eats."

On my survey, I asked people to list foods on their Thanksgiving menu that are tied to their cultural identity. Jan Kristo identified herself as "Lithuanian (Full Blood)." She wrote that "We had headcheese for Thanksgiving—a huge gray loaf substance with pig's feet and knuckles mixed with gelatin. Sounds gross, but I still like it!" Their Thanksgiving meal also included horseradish and herring and "potato fudge" and *ausukes*. According to Jan, potato fudge "has a bottom layer of potatoes and confectionery sugar and a top layer of deep, dark bitter chocolate—so you have the taste of bitter and sweet." *Ausukes* are a "fried dough—we called them 'pig's ears'—in the shape of a bow covered with confectionery sugar, so when you bite into it you either inhale all the sugar and go into a coughing fit or the sugar all goes down the front of you in a blizzard! Eating those successfully was a talent!"

Sorren Varney grew up in Puerto Rico and celebrated in Fajardo with friends of her family. They ate turkey, stuffing, gravy, sweet potatoes, white potatoes, turnips, green beans, cranberries, pumpkin

Cooking turkeys in an *imu*, a large pit oven, is a Thanksgiving tradition in Hawaii. Kiawe wood is used to heat lava rocks that are covered with banana tree stumps. The hot rocks and stumps create steam to cook the turkeys, which are wrapped in foil and placed on the stumps. The turkeys are covered with banana and ti leaves to create more steam and flavor. Next comes a layer of burlap bags and canvas tarps. Finally the *imu* is covered with a large plastic sheet that is sealed tight around the edges by dirt. As a fund-raising activity, schools and community groups build large *imus* and cook Thanksgiving turkeys. Working in a cloud of steam, Koa Lyu, right, and Kai Hovey are putting foil-wrapped turkeys in the *imu*.

pie, and pecan pie—plus *arroz e gandules* (rice and pigeon peas) and pig cooked on a spit. Evie Small Hohler is Jewish, and along with the traditional Thanksgiving meal, her family eats chicken livers, herring, and lox with crackers as an appetizer. During her childhood, Diana Chen's Chinese American family added fried rice, egg rolls, and hot and sour soup to their traditional Thanksgiving dinner. Judith V. Quinn grew up in a Hungarian American family that added stuffed cabbage to the menu.

Kevin Abanilla wrote that he is Filipino, and his family eats *pancit molo,* a soup with wonton wrappers stuffed with a filling, at Thanksgiving. J. J. Johnson identifies himself as West Indian. When he was a kid, his family added red kidney beans, coconut tart, and guava tart to their traditional Thanksgiving dinner. "Baby marshmallows on top of sweet potatoes and Jell-O" were the foods that Rhian Miller listed as reflecting her cultural heritage as a "WASP [White Anglo-Saxon Protestant] Midwestern." A Syrian American person recalled eating *yebedet* (grape leaves with rice and lamb). A Korean American woman wrote that she serves rice and kimchi because her "parents can't eat without kimchi."

Myra Zarnowski remembered the first time she spent Thanksgiving with her Polish American husband's family. "After we ate the turkey and stuffing and all the side dishes, I thought we were

A farmer and his helpers preparing to go to market with goods for Thanksgiving. *Thanksgiving Day—Ways and Means* appeared in *Harper's Weekly,* November 27, 1858.

through. But we were just getting started because then they started bringing out all the Polish dishes—kielbasa, pierogi, etc."

Thanksgiving in Pauline Moley's Italian American family consisted of two meals—one the traditional turkey dinner, the other a complete Italian dinner. For the traditional Thanksgiving meal, Moley listed roast turkey, sage bread stuffing, shrimp-based bread stuffing or oyster stuffing (depending on the favorite of the cook); mashed potatoes; candied sweet potatoes and mashed sweet potatoes; two Jell-O salads (lime Jell-O with carrots and celery and black cherry Jell-O with bing cherries in the bottom, both with whipped cream cheese on top); fresh cranberries and canned

In the mid-1950s, these Seminole women in Florida served a Thanksgiving dinner that included wild turkey and venison.

cranberries; some type of vegetable casserole such as green beans with mushroom soup or cauliflower, broccoli, and brussels sprouts with cheese sauce; and pumpkin pie and pecan pie, both served with freshly whipped cream.

The traditional Italian meal, according to Moley, "usually consisted of homemade ravioli in the traditional red sauce; homemade meatballs (every family member had their special way of making the meatballs); Italian sausage (made by my father, who owned a grocery store and had his own recipe—every Italian grocer had a unique recipe that was secret and guarded); roast, such as chuck or rump, that was stuffed with garlic and mint by chopping the garlic and mint and using a paring knife to make slits throughout the roast and inserting the garlic and mint mixture (the roast was first browned in a skillet on all sides and cooked the rest of the way in a sauce—again to add flavor to the sauce; you can only imagine the size of the pot and the amount of the sauce); salad; Italian bread, not just any bread but, again, bread bought from an Italian bakery."

## Changes

Although some people may be surprised to read about all these modifications in the Thanksgiving menu, there have been many changes throughout the years. For example, celery was once considered indispensable. In 1779, Juliana Smith wrote a letter to her cousin Betsey Smith and described the first appearance of "Sellery" at her family's Thanksgiving feast: "There was an abundance of good Vegetables of all the old Sorts & one which I do not believe you have yet seen. Uncle Simeon had imported the seede from England. . . . It is called Sellery & you eat it without cooking.

It is very good served with meat. Next year Uncle Simeon says he will be able to raise enough to give us all some." By the mid-1800s, it was a staple of the feast, served in a celery glass, a special holder that was prominently displayed on the table. Today, however, celery has been relegated to the relish tray, along with green and black olives, and sometimes carrots and scallions.

A huge chicken pie is another food that was once a main feature of the Thanksgiving Day feast. "This pie," wrote Sarah Josepha Hale, "which is wholly formed of the choicest parts of fowls, enriched and seasoned with a profusion of butter and pepper, and covered with an excellent puff paste, is, like the celebrated pumpkin pie, an indispensable part of a good and true Yankee Thanksgiving." By the early 1900s, few Thanksgiving feasts included a chicken pie, in part because it had been nudged out by the roast turkey.

## Pumpkins and Pies

Some foods, of course, including "the celebrated pumpkin pie," have been on the menu since the 1600s. According to Diane Karter Appelbaum, the English ate pumpkins, or pompions as they called them, "at nearly every meal and in every possible preparation." An early American folk song contained these two lines of verse:

> We have pumpkin at morning and
>     pumpkin at noon,
> If it was not for pumpkin, we should
>     be undone.

Pies, any pies, have always been an important part of Thanksgiving. In his account of being a boy in the mid-1800s, essayist

Charles Dudley Warner described a Thanksgiving when they had twenty-four pies. Harriet Beecher Stowe described pie making for Thanksgiving in her novel *Oldtown Folks*:

> Pies were made by forties and fifties and hun-
> dreds, and made of everything on the earth and
> under the earth. . . . Pumpkin pies, cranberry pies,
> huckleberry pies, cherry pies, green-currant pies,
> peach, pear, and plum pies, custard pies, apple
> pies, Marlborough-pudding pies,—pies with top
> crusts, and pies without—pies adorned with all
> sorts of fanciful flutings and architectural strips
> laid across and around.

Writing about food and Thanksgiving, of course, raises the question: Who does all the cooking?

## Chores

In the late 1600s and early 1700s, preparing for Thanksgiving was typically a family affair, in which the chores were divided according to gender. The men would hunt and chop wood for the cooking fire, and the women would prepare and cook and serve the food and clean up. Children did a variety of chores, including gathering sticks for the fire and nuts for the feast. By the mid-1700s, as people began to buy food and men worked away from the home, women did most of the work for Thanksgiving. In some middle-class homes, the women were assisted by servants.

Throughout these years, children helped in a variety of ways. According to Charles Dudley Warner's account: "For days and days before Thanksgiving the boy was kept at work evenings

This sketch of a family preparing food for Thanksgiving appeared in George Augustus Sala's book about his travels in America in the late 1870s.

[helping to make pies], pounding and paring and cutting up and mixing (not being allowed to taste much), until the world seemed to him to be made of fragrant spices, green fruit, raisins, and pastry,—a world that he was only allowed to enjoy through his nose. How it filled the house with the most delicious smells."

Today, many young children make Thanksgiving decorations for their home. Older children help with setting the table and cooking and cleaning up. Annie Unverzagt wrote that all four of her children "shared in cooking and cleaning up" on Thanksgiving Day. Rachel Nagin wrote that "While my grandmother usually cooks, we all are assigned different side dishes and desserts."

## Cooking

In the late 1980s, Melanie Wallendorf and Eric J. Arnould, professors of marketing and consumer sciences, conducted a systematic study of Thanksgiving Day celebrations in America and found that much of the work is done by women. Even before the actual day, many women are busy cleaning the house, preparing rooms for guests, ironing napkins and tablecloths, polishing silverware, getting out the good china, and doing food shopping and preparation. On Thanksgiving Day, according to Wallendorf and Arnould, "Almost half (42.5 percent) of women surveyed said their major Thanksgiving Day activity is cooking for others, while less than one-quarter (23.9 percent) of men so indicated."

Amanda Tiffany's grandfather is one of those men who cooks on Thanksgiving. "Every year my grandfather creates a gourmet meal. The menu items usually are new twists on traditional dishes. For example, parsnips with mashed potatoes." Since about 1980, Ralph Emer has cooked Thanksgiving dinner. His wife, Dot, reported that "we have this feast at our daughter's house in California—it's a weeklong event. I clean and arrange the house, while Ralph cooks every day. Every year we have to buy some sort of unusual pot, pan, serving dish, or cooking tool. Also, every year there will be one ingredient which is hard to find—persimmons one year, star anise last year."

In my house, we start cleaning and shopping days ahead of time. The night before Thanksgiving, we bake a pumpkin pie, a pecan pie, and a chocolate torte and make a sweet potato casserole, a cranberry relish, and cranberry sauce. On Thanksgiving Day, I

Thanksgiving
November 24, 2005

Roast Turkey
with Herbed Bread Stuffing
and Turkey Giblet Gravy

Persimmon Cranberry Sauce

Potato Parsnip Purée

Green Beans with Lemon and
Pine Nuts

Sweet Potato Brûlée

Creamed Onions

Rutabaga Purée

Sweet Potato Pie with Gingersnap
Pecan Crust

Pumpkin Spice Bundt Cake with
Buttermilk Icing

Ralph Emer's menu for Thanksgiving Day, 2005.

focus on making my special stuffing, which includes chopping and sautéeing broccoli stems, carrots, celery, and pecans. I stuff and cook the turkey. As our grown children and their families arrive along with friends and other relatives, everyone pitches in—paring the potatoes, making the cheese sauce for the broccoli, stirring the gravy. A family who regularly spends Thanksgiving with us brings a tray of samosas, an Indian pastry filled with potatoes and peas and spiced with cardamom.

Food—both old standbys and new creations—is, for many people, the essence of Thanksgiving. "I love the food," wrote Kaliopi Galiatsatos. "It is the only day of the year where dinner is allowed to begin at four and last three hours!" wrote Danny Rothbard. "Food makes people happy," wrote Christina Stine.

# EIGHT

# MANY MEANINGS

On my survey, I asked people to "add anything else you feel/think/know about Thanksgiving." As I read their comments, three themes emerged about the meaning of the holiday.

## Three Themes

The first and most frequently noted theme was about sharing the day with friends and family. "Thanksgiving is a time when family and friends spend time with each other and enjoy life," wrote Nihlas Anderson, a teenager in Florida.

The second theme is about giving thanks. "It's a special time to give thanks for ALL we have," wrote Alissa Seoane, who spends Thanksgiving with relatives in Maspeth, New York.

The third theme is about food. "Thanksgiving is a holiday . . . to share in the harvest foods and to be thankful for our bounty together," wrote Joyce Ruggieri, a teacher in New York City.

All these themes can be connected to the origins—two very old traditions and a very determined woman—of the Thanksgiving that we celebrate today. The theme of giving thanks, specifically to God, was the purpose of the proclamations of days of thanksgiving

Thanksgiving Day has had many meanings throughout American history. Four years after the end of the Civil War, Thomas Nast, a famous and influential political cartoonist, created this cartoon titled *Uncle Sam's Thanksgiving Dinner*. Two symbols of America are depicted at the ends of the table. Uncle Sam carves the turkey, and Columbia, a mythic female figure that symbolizes America, sits between an African American and a Chinese man. People from other countries and a Native American man are seated around the table. At the bottom of the cartoon, Nast expresses the meaning of his Thanksgiving Day cartoon—"Come One Come All" and "Free and Equal."

by religious and civil authorities. Highlighting the bounty of foods, of course, was the basis for the harvest festivals. Sarah Josepha Hale emphasized the gathering of family and friends. She also put forth the ideas of national unity and charity. In 1876, the centennial anniversary of the United States, Hale wrote:

It is a holiday especially worthy of our people. All its associations and all its influences are of the best

kind. It reunites families and friends. It awakens
kindly and generous sentiments. It promotes
peace and good-will among our mixed population.
It gives a festival for the homes of all, and to the
homeless it brings one day in the year of gladness
and plenty. If only for the charitable feeling which
it rouses toward the poor, the suffering, and the
helpless, the day has a value beyond all expression.

Writing this book has made me reflect on a number of things, in particular, the "Pilgrim and Indian" story and a larger meaning of Thanksgiving.

## "Pilgrim and Indian" Story

Although it is not the antecedent of the Thanksgiving that we celebrate today, the "Pilgrim and Indian" story is a true and important story. It is about immigrants' struggle to survive, an indigenous people's decision to help them, and the harvest feast they shared. But there is more—the life of the Wampanoag before the Pilgrims arrived, and the 1621 agreement with rules of conduct and a military alliance between the Wampanoag and English that lasted for many years. The subsequent devastating treatment of Native Americans is also part of the story.

Today, Plimoth Plantation, a museum that was established in 1947 to honor the English colonists, has both English and Wampanoag educational programs, and it is committed to being a bicultural institution. Linda Coombs, associate director of the Wampanoag Indigenous Program, explains: "It is not just a matter of Wampanoag People having the opportunity to tell our 'side' of the story. It is a matter that all of us see the history of the seventeenth century (or of any time period) holistically. There are no sides, but only one whole story."

## Larger Meaning

Sarah Josepha Hale thought about Thanksgiving on a grand scale. She promulgated lofty visions. But, then, she had a mission. For me, however, Thanksgiving was a given, a four-day holiday when we gathered to eat turkey and everything that goes with it. Now that I have immersed myself in the true story of Thanksgiving, I am wondering about a larger meaning, about how to connect Thanksgiving to the world outside my dining room table. One way is to ask questions:

Questions about the food on our table: Where does our food come from? How will climate change affect our food supply? How can we make sure agriculture is sustainable? What can we do about poverty and hunger here and around the world?

Questions about thankfulness: When are we thankful? Just on Thanksgiving? Just when something good happens? Every day? For what are we thankful? Family and friends? Material objects? Good health? A four-day holiday? To whom or what are we thankful—to God, to another person, to luck, to an unknown entity? The people who prepared our feast?

Thanksgiving stamp issued by the U.S. Postal Service on October 19, 2001. Designed by Richard Sheaff, the "stamp honors the tradition of being thankful for the abundance of goods we enjoy in America."

Questions about how we spend Thanksgiving: Preparing the food? Savoring the feast? Going to parades or football games? Watching television? Playing intergenerational games? Talking? Walking? Volunteering at a food pantry or homeless shelter?

Questions about the wider community: How do other people spend Thanksgiving? What do they eat? What do they do? Are they surrounded by friends and family? Are they at the Day of Mourning in Plymouth? Are they involved in an activity that promotes peace and goodwill in the world?

## In Conclusion

All this is part of the true story of Thanksgiving—the origins, the themes, and the questions. It is a much more complicated story than is typically told. But it is a much richer story, a more nuanced and inclusive story, a fitting story for a country that values diversity and openness, a country where we are free to come together any time we please, including on the fourth Thursday of November—Thanksgiving Day.

# Chronology

| | |
|---|---|
| 1541 | Francisco Vásquez de Coronado and his expedition hold a thanksgiving celebration in Palo Duro Canyon in the Texas panhandle. |
| 1564 | French settlers led by René Goulaine de Laudonnière hold a thanksgiving celebration at La Caroline, near present-day Jacksonville, Florida. |
| 1565 | Pedro Menéndez de Avilés holds a thanksgiving celebration in St. Augustine, Florida. |
| 1598 | Juan de Oñate and his expedition hold a thanksgiving celebration near present-day San Elizario, Texas. |
| 1607 | George Popham and a group of English settlers have a thanksgiving celebration with the Abenaki Indians near the Kennebec River in Maine. |
| 1610 | English colonists in Jamestown, Virginia, hold a day of thanksgiving to mark the arrival of a supply ship. |
| 1619 | Newly arrived settlers at Berkeley Plantation hold a service of thanksgiving. |
| 1620 | The *Mayflower*, the ship carrying the English colonists who will settle Plymouth, arrives at Cape Cod. Some passengers go ashore and give thanks at Provincetown, Massachusetts. |
| 1621 | English colonists and the Wampanoag people hold a three-day harvest festival. |
| 1623 | Governor Bradford proclaims a day of thanksgiving for the rain that ends a drought. |

| 1630 | Members of the Massachusetts Bay Colony hold a service of thanksgiving. |
|------|-----|
| 1631 | Governor John Winthrop declares a day of thanksgiving for the arrival of a ship with supplies. |
| 1639 | Civil authorities in Connecticut proclaim an annual day of thanksgiving. Beginning in 1644, an annual thanksgiving day is regularly proclaimed in Connecticut, except in 1675 because of the outbreak of King Philip's War. |
| 1644 | Dutch civil authorities in New Amsterdam (later New York) proclaim a day of thanksgiving. |
| 1693 | The Plymouth church sets apart a day of thanksgiving, April 5, "that the Government over us is yet in the hands of saints." |
| 1777 | The Second Continental Congress appoints one or more thanksgiving days each year until 1784, the year the Revolutionary War ended, each time recommending to the executives of the various states the observance of these days in their states. |
| 1789 & 1795 | President George Washington issues thanksgiving day proclamations. |
| 1798 & 1799 | President John Adams issues thanksgiving day proclamations. |
| 1814 & 1815 | President James Madison issues thanksgiving day proclamations. |
| 1817 | New York State officially adopts Thanksgiving Day as an annual custom. |
| 1827 | Sarah Josepha Hale publishes her novel *Northwood*, which includes two chapters about Thanksgiving Day. |
| 1837 | Sarah Josepha Hale is appointed editor of what would become *Godey's Lady's Book.* |
| 1846 | Sarah Josepha Hale launches her campaign for a National Thanksgiving Day. |
| 1863 | Abraham Lincoln issues two thanksgiving day proclamations. |
| 1877 | Sarah Josepha Hale, at the age of eighty-nine, writes her last editorial on behalf of a National Thanksgiving and retires as editor of *Godey's Lady's Book.* |

1920   The first Thanksgiving Day parade is sponsored by Gimbel Brothers Department Store in Philadelphia—fifteen cars, fifty people, and a firefighter dressed as Santa Claus parade through the streets and Santa Claus climbs a ladder into the Gimbel's toy department.

1924   The first "Macy's Christmas Day Parade" is held on Thanksgiving Day.

1927   Macy's changes the name of its parade to Macy's Thanksgiving Day Parade. Puppeteer Tony Sarg creates the first giant balloons.

1934   The first National Football League game held on Thanksgiving Day is played.

1939   President Franklin Delano Roosevelt changes the date of Thanksgiving from the last Thursday to the fourth Thursday in November.

1941   Congress establishes Thanksgiving Day as an official holiday on the fourth Thursday of November.

1947   The National Turkey Federation starts the practice of giving one live and two dressed (ready-to-cook) turkeys to the president of the United States.

1970   Frank James, known as Wamsutta, makes a speech in Plymouth, Massachusetts, thus beginning the annual National Day of Mourning.

2000   United Nations International Year of Thanksgiving.

2001   Thanksgiving stamp issued by the U.S. Post Office.

# Notes and Sources

Additional sources, reading guide, and the author's Thanksgiving survey are posted on her Web site at www.pennycolman.com.

Abbreviations used are:

DKA—*Thanksgiving: An American Holiday, An American History*, Diana Karter Appelbaum (New York: Facts on File Publications, 1984)

GLB—Sarah Josepha Hale's "Editors' Table," *Godey's Lady's Book and Magazine*

MD—*Red, White and Blue Letter Days: An American Calendar*, Matthew Dennis (Ithaca, NY: Cornell University Press, 2002)

PHM—Pilgrim Hall Museum, Plymouth, Massachusetts, www.pilgrimhall.org

PP—Plimoth Plantation, www.plimoth.org

REF—*Lady of Godey: Sarah Josepha Hale*, Ruth E. Finley (Philadelphia & London: J. B. Lippincott Company, 1931)

SJH—Sarah Josepha Hale

TS—Quotations from the author's Thanksgiving survey

WT—Wampanoag Tribe, www.wampanoagtribe.net

### Author's Note

Dot's and Ralph Emer's quotes are from TS, July 4, 2006.

Sources that tell a different story include: *1621: A New Look at Thanksgiving*, Catherine O'Neill Grace and Margaret M. Bruchac with Plimoth Plantation (Washington: National Geographic Society, 2001); "Deconstructing the Myths of 'The First Thanksgiving,'" Judy Dow and Beverly Slapin, online at www.oyate.org/resources/longthanks.html; and "Thanksgiving," PHM, online at www.pilgrimhall.org.

## Part I

### Chapter 1: The "First" Thanksgiving: Competing Claims

*Sources for table 1: Competing Claims for the "First" Thanksgiving are:*

Coronado's 1541 expedition information in part from Handbook of Texas Online at www.tsha.utexas.edu/handbook/online.

Historical marker information from "Feast of First Thanksgiving," *The Colonial Courier*, April 1960.

"Days of Thanks," Max Albright, *Amarillo Globe News*, online at http://amarillo.com/stories/112599/bel_thanks.shtml.

The Thanksgiving Timeline (TT) in table 1 is online at http://memory.loc.gov/ammem/ndlpedu/features/thanksgiving.timeline.html.

Laudonnière's 1564 expedition information in part from History of Fort Caroline home page, online at www.nps.gov/timu/historyculture/foca_history.htm.

"Influence of France on Florida," Jerry Wilkinson, Historical Preservation Society of the Upper Keys, online at www.keyshistory.org/FL-Fla-Fr.html.

Menéndez's 1565 expedition information in part from History of Fort Caroline home page, online at www.nps.gov/timu/historyculture/foca_history.htm.

*The Cross in the Sand: The Early Catholic Church in Florida 1513–1879*, Michael Gannon (Gainesville, FL: University of Florida Press, 1965).

*America's REAL First Thanksgiving: St. Augustine, Florida, September 8, 1565*, Robyn Gioia (Sarasota, FL: Pineapple Press, 2007).

Oñate's 1598 expedition information in part from Handbook of Texas Online at www.tsha.utexas.edu/handbook/online.

"Don Juan de Oñate and the First Thanksgiving," Don Adams and Teresa A. Kendrick, Historical Text Archive, online at http://historicaltextarchive.com/sections.php?op=viewarticle&artid=736.

"The First Thanksgiving (The Pilgrims Missed It)," Pauline Chavez Bent, New Mexico Genealogical Society, online at www.nmgs.org/art1stThanks.htm.

Popham colony information in part from "Before New England," Richard L. Pflederer, *History Today* 55, no. 1 (January 2005). Information about the archaeological excavation available online at www.pophamcolony.org.

"Thanksgiving," *New York Times*, November 20, 2007.

"Colony Lost and Found (Turns Out the Pilgrims Were Tardy)," Ellen Barry, *Weekly Wire*.

1619 Virginia and historical plaque information in part from "The First

Thanksgiving Day," E. G. Pendleton, Jr., *The Colonial Courier* 14, no. 4 (April 1970).

Information about Lyon G. Tyler and the Reenactments from "Early Thanksgiving, With Purpose," Bob Ruegsegger, *The Virginia Gazette*, November 1, 2006.

1985 Presidential Proclamation, "Presidential Thanksgiving Proclamations 1980–1989," PHM, online at http://www.pilgrimhall.org/thanxproc1980.htm.

Massachusetts events information in part from *Of Plymouth Plantation, 1620–1647*, Samuel Eliot Morison, ed. (New York: Alfred A. Knopf, 1952), available online at www.historyebook.org; "Thanksgiving Articles," PP, online at www.plimoth.org/discover/thanksgiving; and "Thanksgiving," PHM, online at www.pilgrimhall.org/Thanksg.htm; previously cited sources in author's note.

Elizabeth Reis's quote from personal communication with author, October 19 and 21, 2007.

*Chronicles of the Pilgrim Fathers of the Colony of Plymouth 1602–1625*, Alexander Young, ed. (Boston: Charles C. Little and James Brown, 1841).

Arthur Guiterman's poem from DKA.

*Sources for quotations in chapter 1:*

"Florida Teacher Chips Away at Plymouth Rock Thanksgiving Myth," Craig Wilson, *USA Today*, online at http://www.usatoday.com/life/lifestyle/2007-11-20-first-thanksgiving_n.htm.

*Historia de la Nueva Mexio, 1610*, Gaspar Pérez de Villagrá, a critical and annotated Spanish-English edition, translated and edited by Miguel Encinas, Alfred Rodriguez, and Joseph P. Sanchez (Albuquerque: University of New Mexico Press, 1992).

Adams and Kendrick from previously cited "Don Juan de Oñate and the First Thanksgiving."

Edward Winslow's letter excerpt is from *A Journal of the Pilgrims at Plymouth*, Dwight B. Heath, ed. (New York: Corinth Books, 1963), available online at www.historyebook.org.

**Chapter 2: Origins of Our Thanksgiving: Two Very Old Traditions**

Information about the origins of Thanksgiving in part from *The Folklore of American Holidays*, 3rd ed., Hennig Cohen and Tristram Potter Coffin, eds.

(Detroit: Gale Research, Inc., 1999); and "Fast and Thanksgiving Days of Plymouth Colony," Carolyn Freeman Travers, PP, online at www.plimoth.org/discover/thanksgiving/fastandthanks.php.

Information about harvest festivals in part from "Harvest Festivals from Around the World," www.harvestfestivals.net/harvestfestivals.htm; and "Wampanoag Celebrations," WT, online at www.wampanoagtribe.net/Pages/Wampanoag_Education/Celebrations.

Gladys Widdiss's quote is from previously cited WT, "Wampanoag Celebrations."

Harvest home lyrics from *All About American Holidays*, Mamie Krythe (New York: Harper & Row Publishers, 1962).

Juliana Smith's description of Thanksgiving from *We Gather Together: The Story of Thanksgiving*, Ralph and Adele Linton (New York: Schuman, 1949).

Thomas Tucker's quotation from DKA.

Thanksgiving Proclamation excerpts from "National Thanksgiving Proclamations," PHM, online at www.pilgrimhall.org/ThanxProc.htm.

Thomas Jefferson's quotation from DKA.


## Chapter 3: Sarah Josepha Hale's Campaign: "Day of National Thanksgiving"

Sources about SJH include REF; *Sarah Josepha Hale: A New England Pioneer, 1788–1879*, Sherbrooke Rogers (Grantham, NH: Tompson and Rutter, 1985); and the author's visit to the room devoted to SJH, Richards Free Library, Newport, New Hampshire. Information about the library and Hale is online at www.newport.lib.nh.us/HaleAw.html.

Quotes about SJH from REF.

SJH's quote about her education from "Representative Women of Our Own and Other Lands, No.1: Life of Sarah Josepha Hale," Ella Rodman Church, GLB, July 1879.

SJH's story about David's cure from REF.

Description of Thanksgiving in SJH's novel *Northwood: Or, Life North and South* (Boston: Bowles & Dearborn, 1827; reprint ed., Freeport, NY: Books for Libraries, 1972).

SJH's quotes about Thanksgiving Day from GLB in July 1859; October 1852; November 1858, 1866, 1869, and 1870.

Quotes by the governor of Oregon, Mrs. Isaac Atwater, transplanted New
    Englander, and a newspaper report from DKA.
Frederika Bremer's quote from SJH, GLB, November 1858.
SJH's grandson's quote from REF.
SJH's letter to Lincoln available at the American Memory Collection, the
    Library of Congress, online at http://memory.loc.gov/ammem.html.
Excerpt from President Lincoln's proclamation from previously cited PHM,
    "National Thanksgiving Proclamations."
SJH's last editorial from GLB, November 1877.
Telegrams and letters to Franklin Delano Roosevelt from "The Year We Had
    Two Thanksgivings," Franklin D. Roosevelt Presidential Library and
    Museum, online at www.fdrlibrary.marist.edu/thanksg.html.


**Chapter 4: The "Pilgrim and Indian" Story**

Sources for my research quest included *The Youth's Companion, Harper's
    Weekly, New York Times, Washington Post, Christian Science Monitor,* GLB,
    and textbooks.
Joyce Ruggieri's quote is from TS, April 25, 2006.
Doubter's quote is from TS, June 7, 2006.
SJH's quote is from GLB, November 1870.
Edward Winslow's quote from previously cited *A Journal of the Pilgrims at
    Plymouth,* Heath.
Source for another interpretation of the arrival of Massasoit and his men at the
    1621 event include previously cited Grace and Bruchac, *1621: A New Look at
    Thanksgiving.*
Alexander Young's footnote is found in the previously cited *Chronicles of the
    Pilgrim Fathers of the Colony of Plymouth, 1602–1625.*
Quotes from "The First American Thanksgiving" from *The Story of the Thirteen
    Colonies,* H. A. Guerber (New York: Eclectic School Readings, 1898).
Description of the warfare between Native Americans and European settlers
    and the emergence of the "Pilgrim and Indian" story comes from
    discussions with David Lewis-Colman, assistant professor of African
    American history, Ramapo College, Mahwah, New Jersey.
Quotes from the *New York Times* ("dusky redskins . . . white people") come from
    "Thanksgiving on Indian Reservations," November 24, 1901.

A. W. Greeley's quotes from "American Thanksgiving Day Borrowed from
Greeks," *Washington Post*, November 25, 1906.

Quote about Massasoit and Priscilla's stew from *Stories of the Pilgrims*, Margaret
Pumphrey (Chicago: Rand McNally and Company, 1910).

History textbooks quoted are *America in the Making: Wilderness to World Power*,
Charles E. Chadsey, Louis Weinberg, and Chester F. Miller (Boston: D. C.
Heath & Co., 1927); and *Colonial America* (New York: The Macmillan
Company, 1935).

Description of school pageant from "Living and Leisure: Thanksgiving," Jane
Cobb, *Washington Post*, November 17, 1940.

Sources about Americanization and Thanksgiving include "As American As
Pumpkin Pie," Karin Goldstein, PP, online at www.plimoth.org/
discover/Thanksgiving/pumkin-pie.php.

Frank James's speech is linked on "UAINE and the History of National Day of
Mourning," United American Indians of New England, online at
www.uaine.org. Information is also available at PHM, www.pilgrimhall.org/
daymourn.htm.

2006 National Day of Mourning Flyer is online at www.uaine.org.

Biographical sketch of Frank James, "Frank (Wamsutta) James, Fighter for
Native Rights," United American Indians of New England, is online at
Workers World, www.workers.org/ww/2001/wamsutta0308.php.


## Part II

A source with archival illustrations from a private collection for chapters 6, 7,
and 8 is "The New England Child's Thanksgiving," Peggy M. Baker, PHM,
online at www.pilgrimhall.org/ThanksChild.htm.


## Chapter 5: Gatherings: Family and Friends

Caleb Raymond's quote from TS, July 6, 2006.

Jennie Lou Fredle Klim's quote from TS, May 16, 2006.

Angie Schumucker's quote from TS, May 25, 2006.

Lydia Maria Child's poem from *A Lydia Maria Child Reader*, Carolyn L. Karcher,
ed. (Durham, NC: Duke University Press, 1997).

"Thanksgiving Song" from *The Works of Henry Ware, Jr.*, Henry Ware, Jr.
(Chicago: Chapman Bros., 1846).

C. H. Rockwell's quote from "A New England Thanksgiving Day Forty Years
Ago," *Harper's Weekly*, December 1, 1894.

Description of celebration in Rome, Italy, from "Gave Thanks Abroad,"
*Washington Post*, November 28, 1902.

May Hawthorne's account from "Thanksgiving in Jamaica, a Yankee dinner
provided amid tropic surroundings," *The Youth's Companion*, November 28,
1895.

R. F. Putnam's quote from MD.


**Chapter 6: Activities: Good Deeds, Parades, and Football**

Source about activities in part from MD and *All Around the Year: Holidays and
Celebrations in American Life*, Jack Santino (Urbana, IL: University of Illinois
Press, 1994).

Quote about laws and Appelbaum's quote from DKA.

Mrs. R. N. Turner's quote from "Thanksgiving Day," *The Youth's Companion*,
November 18, 1875.

Description of vegetable costumes from "Thanksgiving Decorations: Odd
Costumes for Men and Women," *Christian Science Monitor*, November 14, 1912.

Quote by editors of *The Youth's Companion* from "Morality," November 26, 1841.

Poem "Thanksgiving" from *The Youth's Companion*, November 27, 1856.

George Augustus Sala's quote from *America Revisited*, vol. 1, 2nd ed., George
Augustus Sala (London: Vizetelly and Co., 1882).

Julie Hemming Savage's quote from TS, June 12, 2006.

Anne Chang's quote from TS, August 20, 2006.

Union soldier's quote from DKA.

Newspaper editor's quote from MD.

Dot Emer's quote from personal communication with the author, September
30, 2006.

Source for information about football from MD. A source with archival
illustrations is "Thanksgiving Touchdown," Peggy M. Baker, PHM, online
exhibition at http://www.pilgrimhall.org/ThanxFootball1.htm.

M. Jerry Weiss's quote from TS, May 30, 2006.

Meg Ferron's quote from TS, May 24, 2006.

Lisa Rexford's quote from conversation with author, September 5, 2006.

Doris Weatherford's quote from TS, n.d.

Quotes describing Fantastical parade from "On Thanksgiving and Collective Memory," Amy Adamczyk, *Journal of Historical Sociology* 15, no. 3 (September 2002); and DKA.

Celeste Schamel's quote from previously cited Santino, *All Around the Year.*

Quote from leading citizens Robert W. De Forest, R. Fulton Cutting, Leopold Plaut, William Church Osborn, David A. Greer, D. J. McMahon, Frank Masson North, letter to the editor, *New York Times,* November 29, 1911.

Suzanne Hellman's quote, TS, May 13, 2006.

Heather Nevis-Sosnovsky's quote, TS, May 8, 2006.

Amanda Tiffany's quote, TS, n.d.

Julie Hemming Savage's quote, TS, June 12, 2006.


## Chapter 7: Food: Turkey and Lasagna

Source in part from *Giving Thanks: Thanksgiving Recipes and History, from Pilgrims to Pumpkin Pie,* Kathleen Curtin, Sandra Oliver, and Plimoth Plantation (New York: Clarkson Publishers, 2005); and MD.

Thomas DiBacco's explanation from MD.

Sandip Wilson's quote from TS, June 24, 2006, and personal communication with author, October 20, 2006.

Doris Weatherford's quote from TS, n.d.

David Skurnick's quote from TS, May 27, 2006.

Crystal Lewis-Colman from conversation with author, October 29, 2007.

Voula Parliaros's quote from TS, May 11, 2006.

Jan Kristo's quote from TS, June 17, 2006, and personal communications with author, October 23 and 28, 2006.

Sorren Varney's quote from TS, April 25, 2006.

Evie Small Hohler's quote from TS, May 13, 2006.

Diana Chen's quote from TS, May 29, 2006.

Judith V. Quinn's quote from TS, June 14, 2006.

Kevin Abanilla's quote from TS, July 6, 2006.

J. J. Johnson's quote from TS, June 26, 2006.

Rhian Miller's quote from TS, May 18, 2006.

Myra Zarnowski's quote from conversation with author, September 19, 2006.

Pauline Moley's quote from conversation with author, October 11, 2006, and personal communication with author, November 4, 2006.

Juliana Smith's quote from previously cited Linton and Linton, *We Gather Together.*

SJH's quote from DKA.

Charles Dudley Warner's account from *Being a Boy,* Charles Dudley Warner (Boston: James R. Osgood and Company, 1878).

Quote and folk song about pumpkins from DKA.

Quote from Harriet Beecher Stowe's book *Oldtown Folks* (Boston: Fields, Osgood, 1869; reprint ed., Grosse Point, MI: Scholarly Press, 1968).

Rachel Nagin's quote from TS, May 28, 2006.

Annie Unverzagt's quote from TS, May 22, 2006.

Wallendorf and Arnould's quote from "'We Gather Together': Consumption Rituals of Thanksgiving Day," *The Journal of Consumer Research* 18, no. 1 (June 1991).

Amanda Tiffany's quote from TS, n.d.

Dot Emer's quote from personal communication with author, September 21, 2006.

Kaliopi Galiatsatos's quote from TS, April 25, 2006.

Danny Rothbard's quote from TS, April 16, 2006.

Christina Stine's quote from TS, n.d.


## Chapter 8: Many Meanings

Nihlas Anderson's quote from TS, July 6, 2006.

Alissa Seoane's quote from TS, May 22, 2006.

Joyce Ruggieri's quote from TS, April 25, 2006.

SJH's quote from GLB, November 1876.

Linda Coombs is quoted from "Holistic History: Including the Wampanoag in an Exhibit at Plimoth Plantation," PP, online at www.plimoth.org/discover/wampanoag-life/holistic-history.php.

Another effort to create an inclusive Thanksgiving is described in "Dakota Datebook, November 27, 2003, 'Thanksgiving,'" online at http://www.prairiepublic.org/programs/datebook/bydate/03/1103/112703.jsp.

# Illustration Credits

p. ii PC; p. 16 Benjamin Sanchez, Mission Trail Association; pp. 17, 18 Berkeley Plantation; pp. 19, 20 LOC; pp. 22, 23 PC; p. 24 LOC; pp. 26, 27 PC; p. 28 Homowo African Arts & Cultures; p. 29 PC; p. 31 LOC; p. 32 PC; pp. 36, 40 LOC; pp. 42, 45, 47 PC; p. 48 LOC; p. 53 LOC; p. 54 Indiana Historical Society; pp. 57, 58 NA; p. 61 PC; p. 63 GL; p. 65 PC; p. 71 MHS; p. 72 NA; p. 75 *Indianapolis Recorder* Collection/Indiana Historical Society; pp. 76, 80 PC; pp. 81, 84 LOC; p. 85 University of Northern Iowa Archives; pp. 86, 88 LOC; pp. 93, 94, 96, 97 PC; p. 99 LOC; p. 101 LOC Prints and Photographs Division; p. 103 LOC; p. 104 MHS; p. 107 PC; p. 109 Farm Sanctuary; p. 112 Richard Walker, Kailua High School; p. 113 PC; p. 114 State Library and Archives of Florida; p. 118 PC; p. 120 Dot Emer; p. 122 LOC; p. 124 U.S. Postal Service.

# Index

(Page references in *italic* refer to illustrations.)